DEVELOPING CREATIVE THINKING SKILLS

BY
R.E. MYERS, Ed.D

COPYRIGHT © 2003 Mark Twain Media, Inc.

ISBN 1-58037-254-6

Printing No. CD-1598

Mark Twain Media, Inc., Publishers
Distributed by Carson-Dellosa Publishing Company, Inc.

TABLE OF CONTENTS

TABLE OF CONTENTS

INTRODUCTION

Developing Creative Thinking Skills is designed to stimulate young people to use their many thinking abilities in ways that will help them to succeed both in and out of school. In order to engage in any of the lessons, your students will have to think. We urge you to encourage them to genuinely stretch their minds in responding to the prompts.

The units of this book are organized in an unconventional way for a social studies book. They could have been placed under the headings *Civics*, *Geography*, *Contemporary Issues*, *Sociology*, *Psychology*, *Ethics*, and *Futurism*. These subjects are dealt with in the questions posed to the students. Often, however, the units will have elements of two or more subjects. For instance, when teachers teach history and geography, they find that the two subjects are inseparable. By scanning the list of topics in the Table of Contents, you will readily note the wide range. We sincerely hope that these topics will give you ideas for enlivening your curriculum and motivating your students to think.

We recommend that you read the units that interest you. As you do, you will note that not only is there a wide range of topics in the book, but also that the levels of complexity and difficulty vary considerably from unit to unit. By offering such variety, we have endeavored to allow you to tailor the material to the abilities and backgrounds of your students. In addition to selecting units that seem best suited to your curriculum and students, we urge you to modify any of the units that can profit from your altering, deleting, or expanding them. You are the best judge of how appropriate any of the ideas will be for your students.

By examining the chart that follows, you can note which specific creative and critical thinking skills are fostered in the lessons.

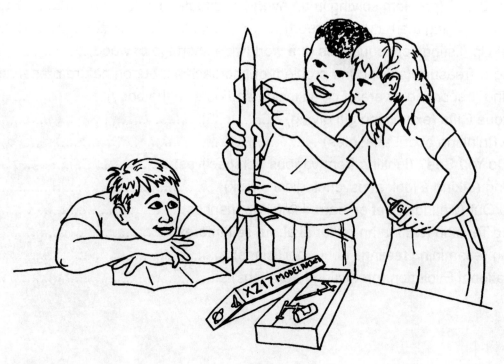

THINKING SKILLS CHART

THINKING SKILLS EMPHASIZED IN THE UNITS

UNITS	Hypothesizing (HY)	Making Judgments (JU)	Analyzing (AN)	Orienting to the Future (OF)	Letting Humor Flow (H)	Breaking Through/Extending Boundaries (BT)	Visualizing Inside (VI)	Looking at It in Another Way (LAW)	Making It Swing, Making It Ring (SR)	Enjoying and Using Fantasy (EF)	Visualizing Richly and Colorfully (VRC)	Combining and Synthesizing (CS)	Putting Ideas Into Context (PIC)	Being Aware of Emotions (AE)	Keeping Open (KO)	Elaborating (E)	Highlighting the Essence (HE)	Being Original (O)	Being Flexible (F)	Producing Alternatives (PA)	Being Sensitive/Finding the Problem (S)
1. Five Folks		X	X											X	X				X		X
2. Sometimes It Works Both Ways	X	X	X	X				X													
3. For a Lifetime	X	X	X	X				X													
4. Where Do They Belong?		X	X									X	X			X					
5. Stated Another Way		X	X													X		X			
6. Campaign Songs		X	X						X			X						X			
7. Presents		X	X										X								
8. Exploring		X	X										X								
9. Election Night		X	X			X													X		
10. Surprises	X	X	X	X																	
11. To the Sheep Barn		X	X				X				X										
12. Hot Chutes		X	X									X				X					
13. Our Twin	X	X	X	X							X										X
14. What Can You Do?		X	X																X		
15. Waiting for the Mail		X	X																	X	
16. Band-Aids Abandoned		X	X																		X
17. Sensible Foolishness		X	X					X					X								
18. Vocations		X	X					X										X			
19. My Favorite Thing	X	X	X																		
20. Beep-Beep!	X	X	X		X																X
21. All Together Now		X	X			X						X									X
22. A Long-Tailed Story	X	X	X		X																X
23. Kuh-whee		X	X							X	X					X					

THINKING SKILLS CHART

THINKING SKILLS EMPHASIZED IN THE UNITS

Thinking skills (column abbreviations):
HY = Hypothesizing · JU = Making Judgments · AN = Analyzing · OF = Orienting to the Future · H = Letting Humor Flow · BT = Breaking Through/Extending Boundaries · VI = Visualizing Inside · LAW = Looking at it in Another Way · SR = Making it Swing, Making it Ring · EF = Enjoying and Using Fantasy · VRC = Visualizing Richly and Colorfully · CS = Combining and Synthesizing · PIC = Putting Ideas Into Context · AE = Being Aware of Emotions · KO = Keeping Open · E = Elaborating · HE = Highlighting the Essence · O = Being Original · F = Being Flexible · PA = Producing Alternatives · S = Being Sensitive/Finding the Problem

UNITS	HY	JU	AN	OF	H	BT	VI	LAW	SR	EF	VRC	CS	PIC	AE	KO	E	HE	O	F	PA	S
24. Stretching Out	X	X	X	X													X				
25. Moving		X	X	X		X				X					X						X
26. Initials at Work		X	X	X			X											X			
27. The Problem of Poverty		X	X	X					X												X
28. Shoes		X	X	X				X						X							
29. Canine Thinking		X	X	X						X											X
30. Circle Back to Fish Camp		X	X	X									X					X			
31. Product Improvement	X	X	X	X							X			X							X
32. Let's Save			X	X															X		X
33. A Town's Dilemma			X	X																	X
34. At the Right Time			X	X											X						X
35. Monthly Puzzles			X	X															X		
36. Elephants			X	X								X							X		
37. Interiors			X	X					X												
38. Community Workers	X	X	X	X											X					X	
39. Ka-boom	X	X	X	X						X					X						
40. The Pilfered Painting			X	X						X							X				X
41. All Even	X	X	X	X		X									X						
42. Public Information	X	X	X	X		X									X						
43. Cheating	X	X	X	X											X						X
44. Burgeoning Barristers	X	X	X	X						X											X
45. The Clowns		X	X	X		X	X														
46. Fooling the Fuzz	X	X	X	X			X							X					X		

THINKING SKILLS CHART

THINKING SKILLS EMPHASIZED IN THE UNITS

UNITS	Hypothesizing (HY)	Making Judgments (JU)	Analyzing (AN)	Orienting to the Future (OF)	Letting Humor Flow (H)	Breaking Through/Extending Boundaries (BT)	Visualizing Inside (VI)	Looking at It in Another Way (LAW)	Making It Swing, Making It Ring (SR)	Enjoying and Using Fantasy (EF)	Visualizing Richly and Colorfully (VRC)	Combining and Synthesizing (CS)	Putting Ideas Into Context (PIC)	Being Aware of Emotions (AE)	Keeping Open (KO)	Elaborating (E)	Highlighting the Essence (HE)	Being Original (O)	Being Flexible (F)	Producing Alternatives (PA)	Being Sensitive/Finding the Problem (S)
47. No Contest!			X	X		X				X				X				X			X
48. True or False?			X	X														X	X		X
49. J.F.M.			X	X																X	X
50. Wasting Away			X	X						X				X				X	X		X
51. Music on the Job			X	X						X	X		X						X		
52. The Things People Say			X	X		X													X		
53. Black or Blue?			X	X										X	X			X			X
54. Greed			X	X										X	X						X X
55. Using It Up			X	X				X													
56. Spoiling a Treasure			X	X				X												X	
57. Sleuthing			X	X																	X X
58. Gratuitous Gifts			X	X									X	X					X		X
59. Poison			X	X						X				X			X	X			X
60. What Do You See?			X	X						X				X			X			X	X
61. Shocking			X	X										X							
62. Locked Out			X	X											X				X		X
63. Relaxed Tension			X	X						X									X		X
64. Emotion		X	X	X											X						
65. Occupational Evolution		X			X																

3

Name: _____   Date: _____

1. FIVE FOLKS

A. Here are five people:

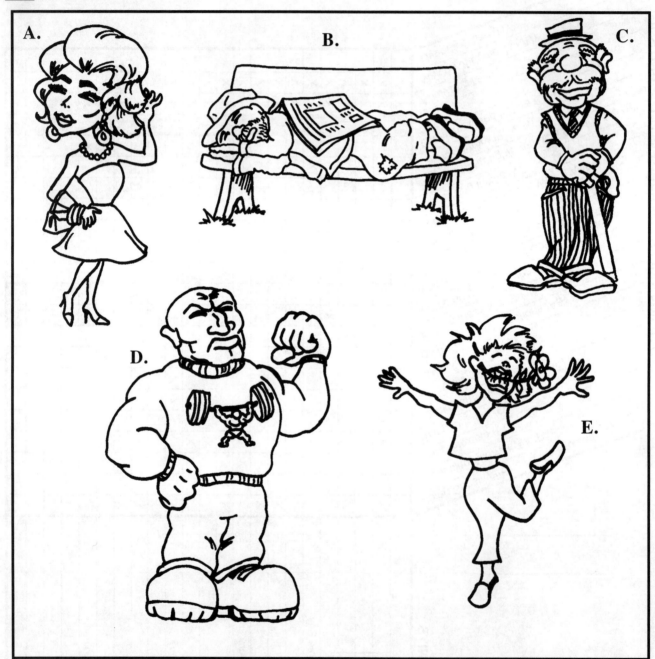

1. Which one doesn't wear socks? _____

Why do you think so? _____

_____

Name: _____ Date: _____

1. FIVE FOLKS

2. Which one, in your opinion, likes to play checkers? _____

   Why do you think so? _____

   _____

   _____

3. Which one makes candy at home every day?

   Why do you think so? _____

   _____

   _____

4. Which one has never owned a pet? _____

   Why do you think so? _____

   _____

   _____

5. In your opinion, which one wears green on Sundays? _____

   Why do you think so? _____

   _____

   _____

6. Which one of the five can't say "library" correctly? _____

   Why do you think so? _____

   _____

   _____

Name: _____ Date: _____

1. FIVE FOLKS

7. Which person tells lies to little kids? _____

Why do you think so? _____

_____

_____

8. Which one likes vanilla ice cream better than chocolate ice cream? _____

Why do you think so? _____

_____

_____

9. Which one likes old movies? _____

Why do you think so? _____

_____

_____

B. How much can you really tell by a person's appearance? Could you be wrong about any of your guesses? Which guesses are you unsure about? Write your second guesses in parentheses, and then ask a friend what he or she thinks. Circle the questions you'd like to know the answers to.

C. Which of the five folks would you like to know? Would you like to know <u>all</u> of them? Why or why not?

_____

_____

_____

_____

Ask your friend which one(s) he or she would like to know. Make a red mark under the ones you agree about.

Name: _____ Date: _____

2. SOMETIMES IT WORKS BOTH WAYS

A. Mr. Ling didn't usually accompany his wife shopping, but on this particular Monday, he thought that he'd be sociable and go to the city's big department store with her. A 24-hour storewide sale for special customers was going on, and Mrs. Ling wanted to buy "one or two things." Since his wife was an avid shopper and occasionally a foolish one, Mr. Ling also wanted to keep an eye on the sales receipts.

Arriving only an hour before the end of the sale (Mr. Ling had purposely delayed their departure for as long as he could), the couple approached a counter, and Mrs. Ling saw a very attractive blouse. She reached into her purse, but to her dismay, found that she had forgotten the coupon that would allow her to get a 20% discount. Going back home was out of the question, because it was a 30-minute drive to their house. Mrs. Ling was terribly upset.

As fate would have it, just as he and his wife were about to leave the store, Mr. Ling glanced down and saw on the floor an envelope like the one his wife had forgotten. Opening it up, he saw that a coupon was inside. Mrs. Ling could now buy whatever she wanted at a 20% discount. For Mr. Ling, finding the coupon was indeed a mixed blessing.

You have probably had a few experiences similar to Mr. Ling's, when an apparent good stroke of luck had some elements that weren't so fortunate. Examine the following situations and tell how they could also be mixed blessings.

1. being given a dog with a pedigree _____

_____

_____

2. being a very good piano player _____

_____

_____

2. SOMETIMES IT WORKS BOTH WAYS (CONT.)

3. winning $2,000 in a lottery _____

_____

_____

4. accidentally striking oil in your backyard _____

_____

_____

5. being awarded a scholarship to a nearby college _____

_____

_____

6. being the only one in your group with a driver's license _____

_____

_____

B. There will be many developments in the future that will change the way in which we live. Some will seem like a boon—but upon further reflection may turn out to be a mixed blessing. A number of people, for example, think television is a mixed blessing. Take a good look at the predicted developments that are listed below, and then tell what you think the advantages and disadvantages might be. Choose the one that you think is most important or most interesting.

Predicted Developments

- a 20-hour work week
- automated assembly lines for cars, trucks, and other vehicles
- twice as many people living on Earth during the next century
- the warming of the earth because of the increasing amounts of carbon dioxide in the atmosphere
- rapid depletion of oil reserves
- ordering goods and services through your home television set
- increasing inflation in industrialized countries at accelerating rates

Name: _____ Date: _____

2. SOMETIMES IT WORKS BOTH WAYS (CONT.)

Disadvantages

_____

_____

_____

_____

_____

Advantages

_____

_____

_____

_____

_____

_____

C. Now that you have given some thought as to what you think might be the advantages and disadvantages of the development, look into it more thoroughly. Research the subject. Then, using the information you will gather about the predicted development, write a research report of your findings. Guidelines for doing your research follow.

2. SOMETIMES IT WORKS BOTH WAYS (CONT.)

Research Guidelines

A. READ

✔ Read carefully. Take notes on points that you think are particularly important.

B. THINK

✔ Don't believe everything you read. Incorrect and misleading information is sometimes found in print. Examine what you read with a critical eye.

C. CHECK

If what you read seems implausible or illogical, try to determine how valid it is by:

✔ comparing it with other sources of information,

✔ deciding how reliable the material is by learning the qualifications of the author or editors,

✔ examining the date of publication, and

✔ determining how well-supported the material is.

D. UNDERSTAND

✔ Try to grasp the substance of the material you read. If the author has a purpose in presenting his ideas, try to discover what that purpose is. Find someone, such as a teacher, parent, or librarian, who can help you to interpret difficult passages. Try to get an overall idea of your material.

Name: _____ Date: _____

3. FOR A LIFETIME

A. Is there anything of which you can say: "That will be there for the rest of my life"? What about a building? Or a bridge? But how many institutions, services, and conveniences will really be there for the rest of your life? Once we called businesses where gasoline was sold "service stations," but now very few of them offer any service, aside from exchanging your money for the gasoline. Telegrams used to be delivered to a person's front door. How are they delivered now? We still have services, but which of them will last throughout your life- time? Will the following things be delivered to your front door for the rest of your life? Explain why or why not.

1. flowers (and balloons) _____

_____

2. mail _____

_____

3. pizza _____

_____

4. Amway™ and Avon™ products _____

_____

5. newspapers _____

_____

B. Which of these institutions will exist throughout your lifetime? Explain why they will or will not last.

1. schools _____

_____

2. religious organizations _____

_____

3. hospitals _____

_____

4. youth organizations (such as the YMCA, YWCA, CYO, Scouts, etc.) _____

_____

Name: _____ Date: _____

3. FOR A LIFETIME (CONT.)

5. libraries _____

_____

6. prisons _____

_____

7. animal shelters, SPCA, pounds, etc. _____

_____

C. Which of these conveniences will be available to you throughout your lifetime? Explain why or why not.

1. telephones _____

_____

2. hair dryers _____

_____

3. calculators _____

_____

4. cameras _____

_____

5. videotape recorders _____

_____

6. music boxes _____

_____

7. microwave ovens _____

_____

8. credit cards _____

_____

9. quartz watches _____

_____

Name: _____ Date: _____

3. FOR A LIFETIME (CONT.)

D. Which of these pastimes will endure throughout your lifetime? Explain why they will or will not.

1. fishing _____
   _____

2. watching television _____
   _____

3. hiking and backpacking _____
   _____

4. motorcycle riding _____
   _____

5. skateboarding _____
   _____

6. social dancing _____
   _____

8. stamp collecting _____
   _____

9. automobile racing _____
   _____
   _____

10. watching professional football _____
    _____
    _____

11. swimming _____
    _____

Name: _____ Date: _____

4. WHERE DO THEY BELONG?

A. Few of us would want to have a picnic in a bus depot or celebrate Independence Day in March. "There's a time and place for everything," as the saying goes. That may or may not always be true, but we do consider some behaviors and activities appropriate in some situations and not in others.

Here are some activities that people conduct every day. Indicate where they might be properly conducted by selecting one option from each category given on the right. In some cases, you may want to select more than one option for the event.

	day	night	on land	in the air	on water	in private	in public	indoors	outdoors	in the country	in the city	winter	spring	summer	fall	
Holding a political rally																
Confiding a personal secret																
Announcing a scientific breakthrough																
Having a wedding reception																
Dedicating a municipal building																
Playing bridge																
Writing a personal letter																
Purchasing a car																
Listening to a flute recital																

B. Where and when would you <u>never</u> want to ...

1. hold a political rally? _____

2. confide a secret? _____

3. announce a scientific breakthrough? _____

4. have a wedding reception? _____

5. dedicate a municipal building? _____

Name: _____ Date: _____

6. play bridge? _____

7. write a personal letter? _____

8. purchase a car? _____

9. listen to a flute recital? _____

C. Now take those nine activities and put them into a different situation from that in which they are usually done, a context where they might be carried on quite successfully. Describe the context for each of the activities.

1. holding a political rally _____

_____

2. confiding a secret _____

_____

3. announcing a scientific breakthrough _____

_____

4. having a wedding reception _____

_____

5. dedicating a municipal building _____

_____

6. playing bridge _____

_____

7. writing a personal letter _____

_____

8. purchasing a car _____

_____

9. listening to a flute recital _____

_____

Name: _____   Date: _____

 STATED ANOTHER WAY

A.

Frankie became frazzled.

Shirley was suddenly sheepish.

Orville turned ornery.

Myron's mood was morbid.

What do you notice about the four sentences above?

When two or more words in a group of words begin with the same sound, it is called **alliteration**. Some writers are quite fond of the device, while some are a little <u>too</u> fond of it. Here are some statements about three states.

Arizona is awfully arid.

Montana has many mountains.

Oregon's ore isn't all gone.

See if you can make up similar statements about the states below.

1. Alaska _____

_____

2. Nevada _____

_____

3. Delaware _____

_____

4. Arkansas _____

_____

5. Alabama _____

_____

6. Washington _____

_____

16

Name: _____ Date: _____

5. STATED ANOTHER WAY (CONT.)

7. Hawaii _____

_____

8. Maine _____

_____

9. Florida _____

_____

10. Minnesota _____

_____

B. Now pick one of your sentences and write two more alliterative statements about it, without naming the state in the two sentences. For example:

> Arizona is awfully arid.
> Its deserts have been deliberately developed to grow crops.
> Getting water for irrigation worries these Westerners.

Your sentences should make sense, of course. If you don't have enough information about a state, find out about it in a reference book, such as an atlas, or on the Internet.

_____

_____

_____

_____

C. Do you like puns? Some people do, and others don't. Can you find the pun in this activity? What is it?

_____

_____

Name: _____ Date: _____

6. CAMPAIGN SONGS

A. Does anything really annoy you? Would you like to start a campaign to punish people who scrape their fingernails on a chalkboard, for instance? Occasionally, all of us would like to put a stop to something. Here are ten items that may or may not really bug you:

1. Would you like to stop the manufacture of red pencils? Why or why not? _____

   _____

   _____

2. Would you like to stop the serving of vegetables such as broccoli in the school's hot lunch? Why or why not?

   _____

   _____

3. Would you like to ostracize people who wiggle their ears by moving their scalps up and down? Why or why not?

   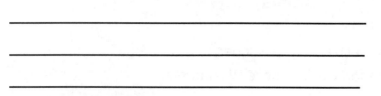   

   _____

   _____

   _____

4. Would you like to stop the sale of black-and-white television sets? Why or why not?

   _____

   _____

5. Would you like to stop the manufacture of water pistols? Why or why not? _____

   _____

   _____

6. Would you like to curb the use of strong cologne? Why or why not? _____

   _____

7. Would you like to ban the assignment of homework until high school? Why or why not?

   _____

   _____

Name: _____ Date: _____

6. CAMPAIGN SONGS (CONT.)

8. Would you like to punish all knuckle-poppers? Why or why not? _____

_____

_____

9. Would you like to prevent photographers from taking pictures of each student at school every fall? Why or why not?

_____

_____

10. Would you like to punish everyone who "cuts" in line? Why or why not? _____

_____

_____

B. What really bugs you? _____

_____

_____

Which campaign would you most like to start? _____

Why?_____

_____

_____

Interview others about their pet peeves and find out how they react to your campaign. Jot down your ideas here.

_____

_____

_____

_____

Name: _____ Date: _____

6. CAMPAIGN SONGS (CONT.)

_____

_____

_____

_____

_____

_____

_____

C. You might need a song to help your campaign along. Think of a well-known melody to which you can put words. You can probably find some sentences in your notes above that will serve as lyrics for your song. You'll probably want to have a rhyme scheme like the one in the song you choose. Try out your lyrics in the space below.

_____

_____

_____

_____

_____

_____

_____

_____

Name: _____ Date: _____

7. PRESENTS

Almost everyone likes to receive gifts—although sometimes we are disappointed in the items we get for birthdays, holidays, or special occasions. Occasionally, however, we receive a gift that is particularly appropriate. We may have wanted it badly, or it may enable us to do something we couldn't otherwise do.

Have you ever thought of what you could have used <u>after</u> you had traveled or had tried to do something new? For instance, have you ever taken a trip and expected the weather to be warm at your destination and found it to be very cold? In a situation such as that, you might have wished that someone had given you a warm coat or sweater as a gift before you left.

If you were a close friend of the following famous people, what presents would you give to them? You should consider what the individual didn't have but would have wanted very much later.

1. What would you have given as a going-away present to Columbus before his first voyage to the New World? _____ Why? _____

    _____

2. What going-away present would you have given to William Brewster as he and the Pilgrims sailed for America in 1620? _____ Why? _____

    _____

3. What would you have given to Lewis and Clark before their historic journey in 1804? _____ Why? _____

    _____

4. What would you have given to James Marshall as a Christmas present before he discovered gold at Sutter's Mill on January 24, 1848? _____ Why? _____

    _____

5. What would you have given as a Christmas present to John Sutter before Marshall discovered gold on his property? _____ Why? _____

    _____

    _____

Name: _____   Date: _____

8. EXPLORING

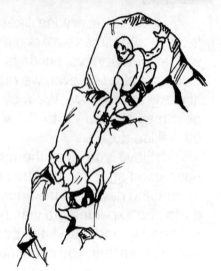

A. People love to explore. They explore outer space, books, jungles, ruins, and all kinds of things. When they do, they usually need equipment, knowledge, tools, companions, and help of various kinds. Do you like to explore? If you have a keen and inquisitive mind, you probably do.

What one thing would you most want to have if you were to explore:

1. a river? _____

Why would you choose that particular thing to help you explore a river?

_____

_____

_____

_____

_____

2. outer space? _____

Why would you choose that particular thing to help you explore outer space?

_____

_____

_____

_____

_____

3. a library? _____

Why would you choose that particular thing to help you explore a library?

_____

_____

Name: _____ Date: _____

8. EXPLORING (CONT.)

_____

_____

_____

_____

4. a mountain? _____

Why would you choose that particular thing to help you explore a mountain?

_____

_____

_____

_____

_____

5. a face? _____

Why would you choose that particular thing to help you explore a face?

_____

_____

_____

_____

_____

6. an underwater grotto? _____

Why would you choose that particular thing to help you explore an underwater grotto?

_____

_____

_____

Name: _____ Date: _____

8. EXPLORING (CONT.)

_____
_____

7. a neighborhood in a city? _____

Why would you choose that particular thing to help you explore a neighborhood in a city?

_____
_____
_____
_____

8. a cave? _____

Why would you choose that particular thing to help you explore a cave?

_____
_____
_____
_____

9. a foreign country? _____

Why would you choose that particular thing to help you explore a foreign country?

_____
_____
_____
_____

Name: _____ Date: _____

8. EXPLORING (CONT.)

10. a mind? _____

Why would you choose that particular thing to help you explore a mind?

_____

_____

_____

_____

_____

B. Which one would you explore tomorrow if you could? _____

Why? _____

_____

_____

_____

_____

_____

C. What needs exploring most in the world now? _____

Why do you think so? _____

_____

_____

_____

_____

_____

_____

Name: _____ Date: _____

9. ELECTION NIGHT

John was excited about the election. It was being held that day in his hometown. His father knew someone who was running for mayor. John wanted Mr. Martin to win. Votes would be counted starting at eight o'clock.

John had to go to bed at nine o'clock, but he wanted to know how the voting was going before he went to bed. The rule in John's house was "no television or radio after eight o'clock." How could John find out about the voting and still obey the rule?

_____

_____

_____

_____

_____

_____

_____

_____

_____

_____

_____

_____

_____

_____

_____

Name: _____   Date: _____

10. SURPRISES

A. Life is full of surprises. Many people are not fond of surprises, however. They like to know what is in store for them, and they are upset when something unexpected happens. On the other hand, life would be very boring if all of our experiences were predictable.

Let's consider some happenings that could be totally unexpected. What would be a complete surprise regarding these local services?

1. public transportation _____
_____

What would your reactions be if this happened?
_____
_____

2. garbage collection _____
_____

What would your reactions be if this happened? _____
_____
_____

3. fire protection _____
_____

What would your reactions be if this happened? _____
_____

4. water supply _____
_____

What would your reactions be if this happened? _____
_____

5. newspaper publication _____
_____

Name: _____ Date: _____

10. SURPRISES (CONT.)

What would your reactions be if this happened? _____

_____

_____

6. mail delivery _____

_____

What would your reactions be if this happened? _____

_____

_____

7. police protection _____

_____

What would your reactions be if this happened? _____

_____

_____

8. library services _____

_____

What would your reactions be if this happened? _____

_____

_____

B. Which of the above unexpected happenings would have the greatest impact upon the community? What would be the results?

_____

_____

_____

_____

_____

_____

Name: _____ Date: _____

11. TO THE SHEEP BARN

A. Have you gone on a short trip lately? You might have taken a stroll to the park or to the mall. You might even have gone to a museum or to a sheep barn to see baby lambs.

People like to travel. Why? To get a change of scenery? To escape? To learn new things? To meet new people?

Why do you go on trips, short or long?

_____

_____

_____

If you had your choice of trips, how far would you go? 5–10 miles? 100 miles? 500 miles? 1,000 miles or longer?

_____

<u>Where</u> would you go if you traveled that far? _____

<u>Why</u> would you go there? _____

_____

Would you like to go with anyone? <u>Who</u> would you like to go with? _____

_____

Why? _____

_____

B. Let's imagine that you do go on the trip. What will you see? _____

_____

_____

Name: _____ Date: _____

11. **TO THE SHEEP BARN** *(CONT.)*

What will you hear? _____

_____

_____

Where will you go when you get there? _____

What will you learn?

_____

_____

_____

C. Draw a sketch of yourself doing what you want to do on your trip.

Name: _____   Date: _____

12. HOT CHUTES

A. Here is a news item that may interest you.

Hot Parachute Stays Up in Air

Dayton, Ohio (UPI)—Research officials at Wright-Patterson Air Force Base have announced the development of a parachute that will keep pilots in the air until they are reached by plane. The new device will be tested during February in California. The parachute pack contains a hot air balloon that is attached to the pilot's main parachute. When the pilot jumps, the regular chute opens with air rushing into the balloon through its vents.

A burner, fed from a tank of propane gas that is strapped to the pilot's back, then ignites and the balloon halts descent, high above the ground, making him or her safe from small arms fire. The balloon would allow the pilot to remain suspended for about 30 minutes, long enough for aircraft to find him or her.

B. The idea that something like a hot air balloon can be added to make a parachute more effective shouldn't surprise you. We have been adding to electronic gadgets, appliances, articles of clothing, vehicles, etc., for a long time. We will most likely continue to do so.

1. What could be added to a post office to make it more picturesque?

_____

_____

_____

2. What could you add to report cards that would make them more appealing?

_____

_____

_____

Name: _____ Date: _____

12. HOT CHUTES (CONT.)

3. What could be added to traffic lights to make them more effective?

_____

_____

_____

_____

4. What might make turnips more interesting?

_____

_____

_____

5. What would make a folk-dancing class in school more colorful?

_____

_____

_____

6. What would make your classroom more colorful?

_____

_____

_____

7. How can you make your next party more colorful?

_____

_____

_____

Name: _____   Date: _____

13. OUR TWIN

A. Suppose a "twin" to our planet is finally discovered in another galaxy and a way is found to reach it. You are among the first intergalactic explorers to visit the planet. It has an atmosphere similar to ours, and its inhabitants are at a stage of civilization comparable to ours. They possess a number of characteristics and technologies that we don't have, but they also lack many things we have in abundance.

B. What would their lives be like if they don't possess a knowledge of how to "harness" electricity? They do have a long history of using steam for energy, fortunately. However, it is against all of the religions of the people inhabiting the planet to use animals for doing work for anyone. All animals are considered sacred, and it is illegal to kill any animal on purpose.

1. How would their homes differ from ours? _____

_____

_____

_____

2. How would their manufacturing differ from ours? _____

_____

_____

_____

3. How would their transportation differ from ours? _____

_____

_____

_____

4. What jobs would be very important in the societies of this planet that do not exist in our developed societies?

_____

_____

_____

5. What would be a good name for this planet? _____

_____

Name: _____   Date: _____

14. WHAT CAN YOU DO?

Let's suppose you are a member of a "knot-hole gang" that attends football games at the university at a reduced rate. You have your ticket and some money to buy pop and a hot dog, and you are anxious to see the game because it is between the university and its chief rival.

Because you live across town from the football field, you are supposed to meet your friends at the school and then leave from there for the game. However, you dilly-dally too long at lunch for that, and even though you hurry, you do not get to the school on time and miss your ride with the others. It is too far to walk, and you do not know how to get to the football field on the city bus. Since it is Saturday, you can find no one at school. You think about phoning your mother and father, but then you realize that they have gone shopping. What can you do?

_____

_____

_____

_____

_____

_____

Have you ever been in other predicaments where you had to use your wits to solve a problem? If so, describe them.

_____

_____

_____

_____

_____

_____

Name: _____ Date: _____

15. WAITING FOR THE MAIL

A. It's nice to get a telephone call from a friend, but sometimes it is even better to get a long letter. After writing a letter, we like to get one back from our correspondent; sometimes, however, we wait in vain. The reply never comes. Receiving a letter can make you very happy, and not receiving a letter can cause you to feel depressed or even furious.

What five persons do you want to hear from by mail (for example, a beloved relative or friend)?

1. _____
2. _____
3. _____
4. _____
5. _____

From which five persons don't you want to receive a letter from (for example, someone asking you for money)?

1. _____
2. _____
3. _____
4. _____
5. _____

From which five persons would you never expect to receive a letter (for example, a sultan of Sarawak)?

1. _____
2. _____
3. _____
4. _____
5. _____

Name: _____ Date: _____

15. WAITING FOR THE MAIL (CONT.)

B. Choose one from each list on the previous page and tell how you would react to receiving each letter.

1. The very welcome letter _____

_____

_____

_____

_____

_____

2. The most unwelcome letter _____

_____

_____

_____

_____

_____

3. The terribly surprising letter _____

_____

_____

_____

_____

_____

_____

Name: _____   Date: _____

16. BAND-AIDS ABANDONED

Without a doubt, the basic cause of the world's most serious problems is overpopulation. Global warming, epidemics, wars, poverty, hunger, and much more are derived directly from overpopulation, in both the so-called "developing" countries and in the industrialized nations. The solutions to poverty and illness and the greenhouse effect that are proposed rarely have anything to do with controlling the earth's escalating birthrate.

Many social problems are approached in a "band-aid" way. We try to stop the bleeding, but we ignore the reasons for the wounds. While there continues to be wounds inflicted, perhaps we should deal with the cause.

The solution of public officials to a city's potholes, for example, is to patch up the roads. Since everyone wants the roads to be safe, their reaction seems reasonable and correct. The contractor who paved the roads may have used inferior materials and/or methods, unfortunately, and the roads will have to be continually patched up. A better approach is to look at the problem with a long-term, rather than a short-term, view and take steps to build roads that won't require constant repairs.

Can you think of an approach to these problems, other than the one being taken now in your community? Take a completely different approach, but one that is based upon your observations of the following problems.

1. Garbage disposal (when landfills are overflowing) _____

_____

_____

_____

_____

_____

_____

Name: _____ Date: _____

16. BAND-AIDS ABANDONED (CONT.)

2. Drunken driving (when tougher penalties aren't reducing the number of arrests and accidents)

_____

_____

_____

_____

_____

_____

_____

_____

3. Students dropping out of school in the ninth and tenth grades (when magnet and alternative schools aren't keeping the dropout rate from falling)

_____

_____

_____

_____

_____

_____

_____

_____

Name: _____   Date: _____

17. SENSIBLE FOOLISHNESS

A. The behavior of people can occasionally be perplexing. At some time, you may have been puzzled by seeing someone behave in a seemingly incomprehensible manner and wondered what was going on.

For example, a man was observed on a Brooklyn rooftop releasing a flock of pigeons. After a half-hour, he set off fireworks, which seemed to be aimed at his pigeons. Moreover, he shouted, whistled, and waved a jacket at them. They appeared to be "homing" pigeons to the casual observer, so shouting and shooting at them didn't make sense. The reason for his behavior was that he was playing a game. His purpose was to keep his pigeons aloft longer so that they might mix with pigeons belonging to others, thus "capturing" them. The game has been played for many decades in Brooklyn.

Have you ever had the experience of seeing someone do something that appeared crazy but really wasn't? If so, what was it?

_____

_____

_____

B. Here are some seemingly foolish behaviors that may not really be so foolish. Try to explain each one.

1. Why does it make sense for a woman to pick up a telephone at 7:00 P.M. and say, "Good morning, honey"?

_____

_____

_____

2. Why does it make sense for a man to light his pipe time after time when he is talking to a gorgeous woman?

_____

_____

_____

Name: _____ Date: _____

17. SENSIBLE FOOLISHNESS (CONT.)

3. Why does it make sense to get dressed up and comb your hair before making a phone call to someone special?

   _____

   _____

4. How could it make sense to get your face and clothes filthy before having a job interview?

   _____

   _____

   _____

5. Why does it make sense for an exhausted accountant to chop wood for two hours as soon as he arrives home from work?

   _____

   _____

   _____

6. How could it make sense for a person to build a big fire in a fireplace when it is 95° outside and 80° inside the home?

   _____

   _____

   _____

7. How could it make sense for someone with a red face and a very bad cough to sit in the front row during a soprano's recital?

   _____

   _____

   _____

8. Why does it make sense to put on your eyeglasses as you start to listen to music on the radio?

   _____

   _____

   _____

Name: _____ Date: _____

18. VOCATIONS

A. For somewhat obvious reasons, teachers have been compared to salespeople, ministers, and actors. Every job, in fact, has features of many other jobs. In this activity, you are asked to think about how four workers resemble people in other occupations. The vocations to be considered are those of the banker, the house painter, the dentist, and the musician.

1. How is a banker like an accountant? _____

_____

How is a banker like a farmer? _____

_____

How is a banker like a police officer? _____

_____

How is a banker like a mail carrier? _____

_____

Who else is a banker like? _____

Why? _____

_____

2. How is a house painter like a hairstylist? _____

_____

How is a house painter like an airline pilot? _____

_____

How is a house painter like an actor? _____

_____

How is a house painter like a newspaper reporter? _____

_____

Name: _____   Date: _____

18. VOCATIONS (CONT.)

Who else is a house painter like?

_____

Why? _____

_____

_____

ALL PATIENTS MUST SIGN IN

CLEAN ME FOR A HAPPY SMILE!

3. How is a dentist like a lawyer?

_____

_____

_____

How is a dentist like a mechanic?

_____

_____

How is a dentist like a stockbroker? _____

_____

How is a dentist like a janitor? _____

_____

Who else is a dentist like? _____

Why? _____

_____

4. How is a musician like a chef? _____

_____

Name: _____ Date: _____

18. VOCATIONS (CONT.)

How is a musician like a carpenter?

_____

_____

_____

How is a musician like a soldier?

_____

_____

_____

How is a musician like a pharmacist?

_____

_____

Who else is a musician like? _____

Why? _____

_____

B. Which of the four workers would you prefer to be? _____

Explain. _____

_____

_____

_____

_____

Name: _____ Date: _____

18. VOCATIONS (CONT.)

C. Perhaps you would like to sum up your ideas about one of the vocations by writing a miniature poem called a **cinquain**. Here is a cinquain that compares teachers to salespeople:

> Teachers,
> Idea sellers,
> Promoting their products
> With prizes, subterfuge, and charm—
> Propagandists.

The cinquain has five lines, and they do not rhyme. Here is a pattern you might follow when writing your cinquain:

> First line - one word, giving the title
> Second line - two words, describing the title
> Third line - three words, expressing an action
> Fourth line - four words, expressing a feeling
> Fifth line - another word for the title

It isn't necessary that you follow the pattern too closely. You might want to vary the length of the different lines or begin the cinquain with a verb rather than a noun. Work out your ideas for your cinquain in the space below.

_____

_____

_____

_____

_____

_____

_____

Name: _____ Date: _____

19. MY FAVORITE THING

A. What is the most precious possession you own? _____

You can tell a lot about someone by asking that question. If you ask a child, what answer are you likely to get?

_____

If you ask a philosopher, he or she might say "brain," "intellect," "experience," or something rather abstract. If you ask a high school student, he or she might respond with anything from a keepsake (an object of sentiment) to something abstract, such as liberty or freedom.

B. Why don't you actually go out and ask some people what they value most? With the exception of a young child, say "most precious possession" each time. If asked to explain, simply say that you are interested in what people really value. (We presume that you are.) Try not to use any other expression unless you are asking a young child. Then you can say, "What thing do you like best?" or "What do you have that you like most of all?"

Try to pick people you don't know or don't know very well. Before you ask the question of the seven individuals listed below, predict the kind of response each will make. You don't have to name the exact thing, just the category (for example, car, toy, talent, jewelry, or valuable possession, something of sentimental and not monetary value, etc.).

	Your Guess	**Individual's Response**
1. a young child (ages 3–5)	_____	_____
2. an older child (ages 6–12)	_____	_____
3. a young adolescent (ages 13–15)	_____	_____
4. an older adolescent (ages 16–19)	_____	_____
5. a young adult (ages 20–35)	_____	_____
6. an older adult (ages 36–64)	_____	_____
7. a senior citizen (ages 65+)	_____	_____

45

Name: _____   Date: _____

19. MY FAVORITE THING (CONT.)

C. Did anyone have the same favorite thing as yours? _____ If so, which one did?

_____

Were you surprised that he or she did? _____ Why? _____

_____

_____

D. Were you surprised by any of the results you obtained from your survey? _____

If so, which ones surprised you? _____

_____

_____

Name: _____ Date: _____

20. BEEP-BEEP!

A little gray-haired lady stopped at the curb across the street from the market. The red light of the traffic signal was shining, so she waited for it to change. As she looked up at the signal, the red light stopped shining, and the green light began to shine. A yellow bus stopped a few feet away on her left, and two cars stopped on her right. Then she stepped down from the curb and took three or four steps.

All of a sudden, she heard "beep-beep!" It seemed to the little gray-haired lady as if the sound came from the bus. She looked at the bus, and she looked at the two cars. The drivers of the cars were not looking at her. She took another step. As she did, she heard another "beep-beep!" This time she knew the sound had come from the bus. Once again, she stared at the bus.

Do you think the bus driver was honking his horn at the little gray-haired lady? If you think so, why was he doing it? If you do not think the bus driver was honking his horn at the little gray-haired lady, where was the sound coming from?

_____

_____

_____

_____

What do you think happened next?

_____

_____

_____

_____

_____

_____

_____

Name: _____ Date: _____

21. ALL TOGETHER NOW

George attends a private school for boys. It is a very competitive school. Twice a year, the students are ranked in each of their classes. A lot of pressure is placed upon the boys by their teachers and parents to excel.

One day, George was detained after class by one of his instructors, so he was late in getting to the long noontime recess. When he came to the playground, he experienced an uneasy feeling. Over at the outdoor basketball court, some boys were playing three-on-three, but they were arguing about fouls as much as they were playing. To the right of them, a game of marbles was being played by four boys in the dirt. One boy was shouting at another boy, who seemed to have the largest pile of marbles. There was a playground supervisor on duty who didn't mind when the boys played "crack the whip." Today, thought George, he should have minded, because the boy at the end of the "whip" of seven had just been sent sprawling and was whimpering about his torn pants and scratched knees.

George had an idea—maybe he could get all of the boys to do something that would be unlikely to cause any hard feelings. What can George do? Think of an activity that would accommodate all of the boys, including George himself. None of the boys that George saw on the playground should be left out of the activity.

_____

_____

_____

_____

_____

_____

_____

_____

Name: _____ Date: _____

22. A LONG-TAILED STORY

Let's suppose that as you are entering a public library, you happen to notice that the man ahead of you is hiding a pet rat in his shirt. No one is aware of the rat in the sleeve of the man's shirt as he takes a seat in a remote area of the reference section. You are a very conscientious and civic-minded person, and you are worried that the rat will escape because the man seems to be falling asleep.

What might happen? What will you do?

_____

_____

_____

_____

_____

_____

_____

_____

_____

_____

_____

_____

Name: _____ Date: _____

23. KUH-WHEE

Kuh-whee is a person. But what Kuh-whee is like is up to you. You can make Kuh-whee any kind of person you would like.

Say "Kuh-whee." What does the name make you think of? _____

_____

_____

Is Kuh-whee a boy or a girl? Or is Kuh-whee a man or a woman? _____

_____

Does Kuh-whee live where it is hot or where it is cold? _____

_____

What kind of clothes does Kuh-whee wear? _____

_____

Where does Kuh-whee live—in a hut, house, or cave? Or does Kuh-whee live on a boat?

_____

_____

Who does Kuh-whee live with? Are there a lot of people nearby? _____

_____

What does Kuh-whee like to eat? _____

_____

On your own paper, draw a picture and show where Kuh-whee lives. Be sure to color Kuh-whee's clothes, eyes, and hair. Show what Kuh-whee likes to do.

Name: _____ Date: _____

24. STRETCHING OUT

A. An athlete extends himself or herself continually in order to improve. The familiar saying in regard to athletic training is, "No pain, no gain." Whether or not you believe this philosophy, we must extend ourselves in order to improve in anything. That includes such diverse activities as dancing, writing, inventing, debating, and mowing the lawn.

Of course, wars have been brought about because countries have extended their boundaries; and extending one's waistline is not usually a good idea. Generally speaking, however, extending oneself physically, socially, and mentally are wise courses of action.

1. What happens when you extend your hand to another person?

_____

_____

2. What happens when you stretch your mind, as in doing a crossword puzzle or math problem?

_____

_____

3. What happens when you extend yourself to the limits of your endurance? _____

_____

_____

4. What happens when you extend yourself to the limits of your patience?_____

_____

_____

B. Think about an area in which you know you can improve but haven't done anything about improving. What is it?

_____

_____

_____

Name: _____   Date: _____

24. STRETCHING OUT (CONT.)

Imagine what your life would be like if you could extend yourself and improve that one area. How would it affect the other parts of your life? Paint a picture—a rather complete picture—of what life would be like if you improve a lot in that area. Describe how it would affect other people in your life—parents, friends, teachers, acquaintances, and others. Before you start writing, though, do some imagining about how you will extend yourself and what the consequences of the added effort will be.

_____

_____

_____

_____

_____

_____

_____

_____

_____

_____

_____

_____

_____

Name: _____   Date: _____

25. MOVING

A. It is said that the average family in the United States moves every three years. If your family is "average," then you've gone to more than one school. Moving, in a way, is scary; but it's also exciting and challenging.

When animals move from one area to another, they have a definite reason for doing so. People do too, but they have many more reasons for changing their residences. What are some of the reasons that people move from one town or city to another?

_____

_____

_____

B. If you have moved from one city or town to another one, what was the main reason for your move?

_____

_____

C. We might compare the migrations of birds, whales, lemmings, reindeer, and salmon to those of people. People move for some of the same reasons.

1. What kinds of people migrate regularly to places where there is more food?

_____

_____

2. What kinds of people migrate regularly to a warmer climate each winter?

_____

_____

_____

3. Are there people who return to the same location to give birth to and/or raise their children? If so, describe them.

_____

_____

_____

Name: _____ Date: _____

25. MOVING (CONT.)

D. Keeping in mind that a migration, generally speaking, involves a large number of individuals, tell why these events might result in a migration.

1. a bank robbery _____

_____

2. a drought _____

_____

3. the construction of a school _____

_____

4. a baseball game _____

_____

5. a war _____

_____

6. the election of a president _____

_____

7. a flood _____

_____

8. knocking down the trees of an orchard to build houses _____

_____

9. a wedding _____

_____

Name: _____ Date: _____

25. MOVING (CONT.)

E. What major changes in our society and on Earth might make us less restless and not inclined to move so often? Think about global as well as national conditions and events that might make moving a rare event.

_____

_____

_____

_____

_____

_____

_____

_____

_____

_____

_____

_____

_____

_____

_____

_____

_____

_____

Name: _____ Date: _____

26. INITIALS AT WORK

A. We know of a painter who signs her work "D. Light." As a matter of fact, her paintings are rather delightful. This made us think about appropriate names for people in various occupations. A referee might have the name "B. Fair," for example. "R. U. Reddy" might be a good name for a dentist or a starter at a track meet. A private detective could have a name such as "C. A. Lott." "K. Dents" could be a drill sergeant, and a sailor might be named "C. Ward." "B. A. Saylor" could be a recruiter for the navy, and a tour-bus driver might even have the name of "C. R. Towne."

B. Let's see if you can come up with names starting with initials for people in the following occupations.

1. realtor _____

2. cowboy _____

3. chef _____

4. thief _____

5. fashion model _____

C. What would be an appropriate occupation for each of the following names?

1. E. Z. Reeder _____

2. I. Block _____

3. I. Ketcham _____

4. Q. Player _____

5. D. Best _____

Name: _____ Date: _____

26. INITIALS AT WORK (CONT.)

6. A. Croker _____

7. I. Lie _____

8. Y. B. Rich _____

9. A. Roper _____

10. X. L. Lantz _____

11. I. M. Wise _____

12. C. C. Wrenn _____

D. Can you think of any other initialed names and occupations that match?

_____

_____

_____

_____

_____

_____

_____

_____

_____

_____

_____

Name: _____ Date: _____

27. THE PROBLEM OF POVERTY

A. A teacher received a number of differing reactions when he tossed out this quotation to a sixth-grade class one day: "Poverty produces foolish generosity."

Except for a few in the class, the students were all from middle-class homes. One boy scoffed at the idea, saying: "If I were poor, I'd rather live than give."

A girl thought that being poor might have something to do with having poor judgment.

Do poor people generally have poor judgment? _____

Explain. _____

_____

_____

_____

B. Since poverty is a serious problem in our country, as well as throughout the world, it might be a good idea to consider the implications of that remarkable statement, "Poverty produces foolish generosity." Can you see any connection between being poor and being foolishly generous? How can the two go together?

_____

_____

_____

_____

_____

_____

_____

_____

Name: _____ Date: _____

28. SHOES

A. We see and hear a lot about shoes. There are many ads about shoes on TV these days. Shoes are really important to people in their jobs. Here are five pairs of shoes that people use in their work. Who wears them?

_____ _____ _____

_____   _____

What kind of shoes do you like best? Draw a picture of them.

B. When you were younger, you may have had fancy laces for your shoes. You may have even had little bells on your shoes that jingled when you walked. Perhaps having shoes that make sounds isn't a good idea, especially for older people. What do you think?

_____

_____

_____

Name: _____ Date: _____

28. SHOES (CONT.)

C. Let's imagine that several men living in a boardinghouse all have different jobs. One of them is a practical joker. When a terrible storm causes a power outage, this fellow sees his chance. There is no electricity, yet everyone still has to go to work on that very dark January morning. The joker gets up early and, with the aid of the only flashlight in the boardinghouse, he switches the shoes of all of the boarders. Here are their jobs with the type of shoes each wears:

 telephone repairman (spiked boots)
 private detective (oxfords with crepe soles)
 accountant (oxfords)
 mail carrier (lightweight oxfords)
 logger (heavy boots)
 dancer (oxfords with metal taps)

Whose shoes were switched around by the practical joker?

_____ with _____

_____ with _____

_____ with _____

What were the results? _____

_____

_____

_____

_____

D. Which one was the practical joker? _____ Why do you think so?

_____

_____

_____

Name: _____   Date: _____

29. CANINE THINKING

A. We often act as if our pets are human, scolding them for being naughty and not behaving in a proper way, when they are actually behaving in a very animal-like manner. When we do this, we are falling victim to man's oldest game, making believe that things that are not human have human-like characteristics and motives. We tend to think that everything in the world is a little or a lot like us. But do you suppose a dog looks at us like that? Or a cat? Do they wonder why we don't behave in a more dog-like or cat-like way?

1. Imagine that you are a cat, and you think that people behave as cats do. You see a brown-haired boy of twelve entering the kitchen. What do you suppose he is going to do?

   _____

   _____

   _____

   _____

2. You see your mistress, a thin, middle-aged lady, pick up a ball of yarn. What do you suppose she is going to do?

   _____

   _____

   _____

3. Imagine that you are a dog, and you think that people behave as dogs do. You see a boy running down the street, trying to catch a bus. What do you think the boy is doing?

   _____

   _____

   _____

61

Name: _____ Date: _____

29. CANINE THINKING (CONT.)

4. You see several children playing "tag." A girl is trying to tag a boy. What do you think she is doing?

_____

_____

_____

B. In what ways would we be better off if we thought like a cat? _____

_____

_____

_____

_____

_____

_____

_____

C. In what ways would we be better off if we thought like a dog? _____

_____

_____

_____

_____

_____

Name: _____ Date: _____

30. CIRCLE BACK TO FISH CAMP

A. Where might you find these towns in the United States? What would be the geographical and topological features of the areas in which they are situated? Explain why the towns have the names they have.

1. Fish Camp _____

_____

_____

_____

_____

2. Rock Hill _____

_____

_____

_____

_____

3. Junction City _____

_____

_____

_____

_____

4. Silverton _____

_____

_____

_____

_____

Name: _____ Date: _____

30. CIRCLE BACK TO FISH CAMP (CONT.)

5. Geyserville _____

_____

_____

_____

_____

6. Snowmass _____

_____

_____

_____

_____

7. Waterford _____

_____

_____

_____

_____

8. Thermal _____

_____

_____

_____

_____

9. Garden of the Gods _____

_____

_____

_____

_____

Name: _____ Date: _____

30. CIRCLE BACK TO FISH CAMP (CONT.)

10. Circle Back _____

_____

_____

_____

11. Curve _____

_____

_____

_____

12. Ceres _____

_____

_____

_____

B. If you had been a pioneer at the beginning of the nineteenth century and had come upon an appropriate site for a settlement, you probably would have wanted to name it. What names would you have given to the following places?

a. The site is at the foot of a range of high mountains, near the entrance of a pass. The land has many boulders scattered over the rolling hills. An all-year stream flows by the site. There are four seasons here, and they are quite distinct.

_____

b. Two prominent trails intersect at this site. There is no stream, lake, or any other water on the surface of the land; but, because a mountain range to the east is only fifteen miles away, it looks as if a well could be drilled and underground water reached rather easily. Located at the edge of a plain, the site has almost no trees and is subject to

Name: _____ Date: _____

30. CIRCLE BACK TO FISH CAMP (CONT.)

violent windstorms and snowstorms. It is very hot here in the summer and very cold in the winter. Nevertheless, because the two trails cross here, it is a good location for a trading post.

_____

c. The site is where two streams come together and then flow northward as a river. The terrain is flat, and the only trees in the area are along the streams and river. Grass grows abundantly in the fields and meadows. There are four seasons, but the very hot weather lasts about three weeks. Snowfall averages four inches a year, according to the Indians who live in the area.

_____

d. The site is at the center of a lovely but small bay on the coast of the Pacific Ocean. Looking inland from the curved shoreline, you see a small sloping hill. The curve of the bay allows for ships to anchor offshore because, except during storms, the water in the bay is very calm. Temperatures are mild all year long. There are only two seasons here—wet and dry.

_____

e. On the east of this site are plains, and on the west are scattered mountain ranges. The site itself is alongside a stream in a basin where streams have no outlet. It is hot and dry to the east and south, but the weather is tolerable in the basin. It is on one of the main routes through this part of the country. When irrigated, the land produces fine crops (mostly vegetables).

_____

_____

Name: _____ Date: _____

31. PRODUCT IMPROVEMENT

A. By adding an element or component, imaginative individuals have often improved the ease and satisfaction with which we accomplish tasks and engage in play. For example, by adding sound to the original silent moving pictures, the people who made movies enabled their audiences not only to hear the voices of the actors, but also to hear the accompanying sounds of the scenes and background music.

Adding music, in fact, usually improves a "live" play or a working environment. Both farm animals and humans seem to be more productive when they have the right kind of music played for them on a radio or sound system.

B. Can you think of products that would be improved by the addition of music? Pencils or pens that had miniature tape recorders would probably be distracting, but there might be other items that would be improved with the addition of music.

Would the following items be improved with the addition of music?

1. shoes _____ What would happen if we had shoes that made music? _____

_____

2. spoons _____ What would happen if the spoons we ate with played a tune every time we used them? _____

_____

3. toothbrushes _____ How would our lives be changed if our toothbrushes played music when we used them? _____

_____

4. bicycles _____ What would happen if music resulted when we pedaled our bikes?

_____

_____

Name: _____ Date: _____

31. PRODUCT IMPROVEMENT (CONT.)

5. flashlights _____ What might be the results if flashlights, when turned on, played tunes? _____

_____

6. brooms _____ What would happen if a broom played a melody every time it was used? _____

_____

7. dog leashes _____ What would be the results if a leash played a tune every time a dog's master put it on the dog? _____

_____

C. Can you think of any products that would be improved by having the capacity to make music? If so, tell how these products would improve people's lives.

_____

_____

_____

_____

_____

_____

_____

Name: _____ Date: _____

32. LET'S SAVE

A. Every day we are urged to save. In newspapers and magazines, on radio and television, and in the classroom, people are asking us to save. Often they recommend ways in which the saving can be accomplished, but it is up to us to decide how we can save the things that are most important to us. If you haven't given saving much thought lately, you may benefit from thinking about saving the various items below.

1. What is the most effective way to save soap? _____

_____

Would you recommend saving it in this way? _____ Why or why not? _____

_____

What is the least effective way of saving soap? _____

_____

Would you recommend saving it in this way? _____ Why or why not? _____

_____

2. What is the most effective way to save clothing?_____

_____

Would you recommend saving it in this way? _____ Why or why not? _____

_____

What is the least effective way of saving clothing? _____

_____

Would you recommend saving it in this way? _____ Why or why not? _____

_____

3. What is the most effective way of saving money? _____

_____

Name: _____ Date: _____

32. LET'S SAVE (CONT.)

Would you recommend saving it in this way? _____ Why or why not? _____

_____

What is the least effective way of saving money? _____

_____

Would you recommend saving it in this way? _____ Why or why not? _____

_____

4. What is the most effective way of saving someone from drowning? _____

_____

Would you recommend that someone be saved in this way? _____ Why or

why not? _____

_____

What is the least effective way of saving someone from drowning? _____

_____

Why is it the least effective way? _____

_____

5. What is the most effective way to save energy? _____

_____

Would you recommend saving energy in this way? _____ Why or why not?

_____

What is the least effective way to save energy? _____

_____

Would you recommend this method? _____ Why or why not? _____

_____

32. LET'S SAVE (CONT.)

6. What is the most effective way to save time? _____

_____

Would you recommend saving time in this way? Why or why not? _____

_____

What is the least effective way to save time? _____

_____

Would you recommend this method? _____ Why or why not? _____

_____

B. Look back at the various ways in which you suggested that things might be saved. What are the different interpretations you made of the word *save*. Name as many as you can find. (For example, "to store up" is one interpretation.)

_____

_____

_____

_____

Now look up the word *save* in the dictionary. Did you cover most of the meanings given in the dictionary? Which ones did you omit?

_____

_____

C. If you are especially interested in saving one of the items on the previous pages—or anything else–why don't you write an essay about why this saving should be done by people? An **essay** is a piece of writing about a particular subject that is written from a particular point of view. Its purpose is to persuade people to do something or to make them feel a certain way. In other words, it is intended to influence people. Present your argument in a clear, concise manner. Support it with anecdotes, examples, and statements by authorities. If you are able to think of counter-arguments after you have finished your first draft, rewrite your essay in such a way as to account for the points that might be raised in opposition to your contentions. Use your own paper to sketch out the main ideas or outline for your essay.

Name: _____ Date: _____

33. A TOWN'S DILEMMA

This is a map of an area surrounding a town that is about one hundred years old. It is located in the Northwest, and it has two neighboring towns, both of which are small. Although its reputation as a lovely and healthy place in which to live is deserved, the town is in a period of serious decline. In the past year, many people have lost their jobs, and the prospect of further layoffs is great.

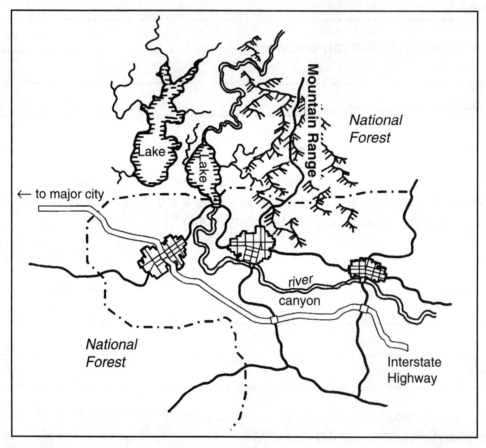

1. What kind of industry supports this town? _____

   _____

2. Why have people been losing their jobs? _____

   _____

   _____

   _____

3. What can the people of this town do to revive it and keep it prosperous? On your own paper, list all of the ways that the economic decline of the town can be stopped or even reversed.

72

Name: _____ Date: _____

34. AT THE RIGHT TIME

A. There are times when it is better to do some things rather than others. For instance, swimming in a river or lake is more fun and safer in the summer than in winter. In most parts of our country, people prefer certain activities over others because of the weather. Although there are ice rinks for ice skaters, people who like to skate and ski on the ice and snow are more likely to think of those sports in the winter. Most of us like to read books when the weather is rainy or snowy.

Here are a variety of activities. Tell which time of year it is best to engage in them and why.

When is the best time to ...

1. sew on a button? _____ Why? _____

_____

2. wash a dog? _____ Why? _____

_____

3. build a fort? _____ Why? _____

_____

4. take a walk? _____ Why? _____

_____

5. barbecue a chicken? _____ Why? _____

_____

6. visit a sick person? _____ Why? _____

_____

7. concoct a new recipe? _____ Why? _____

_____

Name: _____ Date: _____

34. AT THE RIGHT TIME (CONT.)

8. buy a ring? _____ Why? _____

_____

9. paint a picture? _____ Why? _____

_____

10. watch fireflies? _____ Why? _____

_____

11. talk to a cat? _____ Why? _____

_____

12. learn a magic trick? _____ Why? _____

_____

B. Which of the activities above would you like to do right now? _____

_____

_____

_____

_____

_____

_____

_____

_____

_____

Name: _____ Date: _____

35. MONTHLY PUZZLES

During the year, there are many times when you can help others. Sometimes you have to think about what you can do, though. Some months you have a very good chance to be helpful.

1. In August, what can you do to help a dog keep cool without getting it wet?

_____

_____

_____

_____

2. In October on Halloween, how can you have a good time outside without doing any damage to things that belong to others?

_____

_____

_____

_____

3. In November, what can you do to help people who keep the streets clean without making smoke?

_____

_____

_____

_____

4. In December, how can you thank your teacher without giving him or her a present?

_____

_____

_____

Name: _____ Date: _____

35. MONTHLY PUZZLES (CONT.)

5. In January, how can you help your mail carrier without inviting him or her into your home?

_____

_____

_____

_____

6. In February, to whom can you give a valentine? Think of someone who wouldn't get one otherwise.

_____

_____

_____

_____

_____

7. In March, what can you do to make your home less drafty?

_____

_____

_____

_____

8. In May, what can you do to show how pretty the flowers are without picking them?

_____

_____

_____

_____

Name: _____ Date: _____

36. ELEPHANTS

A. The Greenhill Humane Society's newsletter made this strong point recently:

> **Performing Animals—All Work and No Play**
>
> Going to the circus may be a lot of kids' idea of a great time, but the truth is that animals often suffer their entire lives to "entertain" us. The only life a circus animal knows is usually iron bars, cramped cages, training, and confinement. Animals become permanent prisoners—their world consists of performing unnatural and uncomfortable stunts in order to line the circus owners' pockets with money.
>
> Because it is not in elephants' natures to stand on their heads, or on each other, trainers must use cruelty to push them to perform such difficult acts. Animal handlers have been found using steel-line whips, hot irons, spikers, and electrical shocks; and they sometimes fire pistols to frighten animals into learning their routines.
>
> The audience sees animals "happily" skating, jumping through hoops, or doing headstands. After the show, people go home to relax and stretch out, while the animals are herded back to their cells, forgotten after the lights go out.

Do you agree with this opinion? _____ Explain why you do or do not.

_____

_____

_____

_____

_____

_____

_____

_____

Name: _____ Date: _____

36. ELEPHANTS (CONT.)

B. We can never know what's really going on inside an elephant's head, of course. We can only make guesses, based on the animal's behavior. Although elephants are keenly intelligent, they don't speak any human language. They can show their displeasure, however, as we have learned many times from tragedies in zoos and circuses.

If a performing elephant could talk, what do you think it would say? Would it make a difference if the elephant were born in captivity or not? Write several paragraphs of dialogue between the elephant and its trainer.

_____

_____

_____

_____

_____

_____

_____

_____

_____

_____

_____

_____

_____

_____

_____

_____

_____

_____

Name: _____ Date: _____

37. INTERIORS

A. Have you ever passed a house or building and wondered what was inside? Sometimes if you are able to enter that house or building, you are greatly surprised. The inside can be quite different from the outside.

Here are a few dwellings that you might have wondered about from time to time when you have been reading. On your own paper, sketch what you think the inside of each might be like. Label the items you sketch.

A.

B.

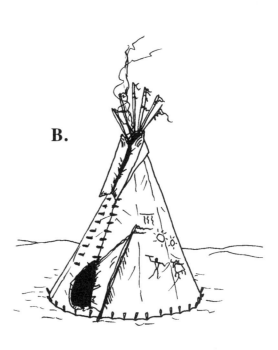

C.

Is the building in C really a "dwelling"? _____ How do you know?

_____

_____

B. Now do a little research. Find out if you were correct about the items that are usually in the first two dwellings and about the furnishings of the third building, which is very famous. Revise your sketch accordingly.

Name: _____ Date: _____

38. COMMUNITY WORKERS

These are some of the workers in your town that help the community:

❖ letter carrier   ❖ police officer

❖ firefighter   ❖ librarian

❖ dogcatcher   ❖ street cleaner

❖ park gardener   ❖ paramedic

1. Is it all right for one worker to do another worker's job sometimes? _____

2. Can you imagine a time when a police officer would act like one of the other workers?

   _____ Which one? _____

   When could it happen? _____

3. Does a librarian ever do the work of any of the other community workers? _____

   Which one? _____

   When could it happen? _____

   _____

   _____

4. Would a letter carrier ever do what another worker does? _____ What might

   the letter carrier do? _____

   _____

   _____

5. Can you think of a time when a firefighter would do what another community worker does?

   _____ When would the firefighter do that? _____

   _____

   _____

   _____

      80

Name: _____ Date: _____

39. KA-BOOM

A. Are you aware of all the explosions that punctuate your life? _____

Did you ever give any thought to your own ability to create explosions? _____

 Some explosions are useful, such as a sneeze or a dynamite blast that removes an obstruction. Many explosions provide us with amusement, such as a popping balloon or a guffaw. Other explosions are characterized by violence and may do great harm, such as the detonation of a nuclear bomb or the explosion of gas in a sewer. There are many kinds of explosions, but all of them are easily identified as explosions. Why? What makes us call something an explosion?

B. Name some explosions that benefit people. _____

_____

_____

_____

_____

Name some explosions that harm people or other things. _____

_____

_____

_____

_____

C. What kind of explosion might result in

1. a detour? _____

2. a formal portrait? _____

3. a television station going off the air? _____

4. soda water spattered over the interior of a car? _____

5. a canceled party? _____

Name: _____   Date: _____

39. KA-BOOM (CONT.)

6. broken windows? _____

7. a youngster's laugh? _____

8. sudden riches? _____

D. Name three explosions that have been of immense benefit to mankind. If none come readily to mind, do some library research to come up with your selections.

_____

_____

_____

_____

_____

_____

_____

_____

Name: _____ Date: _____

40. THE PILFERED PAINTING

A family of four—father, mother, son, and daughter—went to an art fair about forty miles from where they lived. The art fair was situated in the downtown park of a small town. The town wasn't large, but it was famous for its artists and eccentrics. As the family approached a group of paintings on easels set up by a woman in a long shawl, the boy, who was nearly 17, called his mother's attention to an oil painting of a country scene. The painting depicted some tall trees, a brooding, cloudy sky, and two farm buildings. The predominant colors were greens and browns.

After remarking that she liked the painting, the mother was surprised to see her son pull out his camera and take a picture of the painting. As he did so, the artist held out a hand and remonstrated, not too loudly, with the boy for photographing her work; he ignored her. The mother was somewhat embarrassed, so along with the other three, she moved on to the next grouping of paintings.

A. Should the artist have complained about the boy's taking a photograph of her painting? Why or why not?

_____

_____

_____

_____

_____

B. Should the mother and father have offered to compensate the artist for the photograph their son had taken? Explain.

_____

_____

_____

_____

_____

83

Name: _____ Date: _____

C. What are the critical factors involved in the issue of whether or not the boy should have taken the picture?

_____

_____

_____

D. Where can you go to get information about problems of this kind? _____

_____

_____

_____

E. Is this an example of a moral or ethical issue? Why or why not? _____

_____

_____

_____

F. Is this an example of a legal issue? Why or why not? _____

_____

_____

_____

G. What will happen the next time someone takes a photograph of the artist's work? Who is likely to do it? What will her reaction be? Give a complete accounting of the scene and action. Resolve the problem in light of how you answered the questions above. Continue on your own paper.

_____

_____

_____

Name: _____ Date: _____

41. ALL EVEN

A. Balance is terribly important. We need balance just to walk. There has to be balance in nature. If things get out of balance in nature, one species may prosper, but another may suffer. As a practical matter in human affairs, budgets must be balanced—or we pay the consequences.

B. Is this balanced? _____

C. Is this unbalanced? _____

D. Do these need balancing?

1. diet? _____ In what ways? _____
_____
_____

2. daily activities? _____ In what ways? _____
_____
_____

3. neighborhoods? _____ In what ways? _____
_____
_____

4. musical performances? _____ In what ways? _____
_____
_____

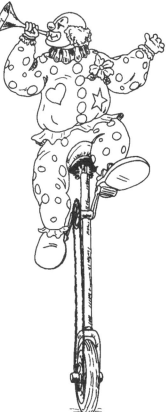

85

Name: _____ Date: _____

42. PUBLIC INFORMATION

A. When you are living in the year 2029, the world won't be the same as it is now. But it is very likely that there will be newspapers so people can find out what is happening locally, nationally, and throughout the world. The newspapers will most likely still publish information that the countries and cities want people to know about. These stories are called public notices.

Here is a public notice that could perhaps be found in a newspaper on May 29, 2029. There are some blank spaces in the notice. Every blank space has a number beside it. There are some words with numbers below the notice. When you come to a blank space, look at its number. Then fill the space with a word from the column that has that number. When you have filled in all of the blanks, finish the notice with one more sentence.

PUBLIC NOTICE

The city fire department will take all of the (1) _____ you can find in your (2) _____. They will be collected at (3) _____, so everyone can enjoy watching them (4) _____ on June 1. _____

_____

_____

_____

1	2	3	4
toys rockets	school house	midnight once	catch fire fly
Christmas trees	car yard	noon 6 o'clock	smoke explode
balloons worms	building	sunrise sunset	melt float
TV games	apartment	gunpoint	wiggle

B. Draw a picture to show what will happen on June 1, 2029. Use your own paper.

Name: _____ Date: _____

43. CHEATING

A. There are a number of actions people take that don't get them arrested but that many of us still consider reprehensible. Some people get away with actions that are on the borderline of illegality or immorality because nearly everyone lets them get away with their behavior. They take advantage of someone, barely skirt the law, or ignore standards of decent conduct.

Which of these actions constitutes cheating? Explain why you take the position that you do concerning each situation.

Is it cheating to ...

1. Sample grapes, plums, cherry tomatoes, and other produce that you don't buy when you are in the market?

_____

_____

2. Reuse a postage stamp that arrived not canceled in your mail? _____

_____

_____

3. Park in a space with a parking meter that has been jammed and can't be operated?

_____

_____

_____

4. Ask someone to help you write a composition for an assignment? _____

_____

_____

5. Or ask someone to give you a word or phrase to use in that composition?

_____

_____

_____

Name: _____ Date: _____

43. CHEATING (CONT.)

6. Write an anonymous "poison pen" letter to someone that is terribly critical of that individual or just downright nasty?

_____

_____

_____

7. Sign a pseudonym to a letter you send to a business complaining about its service?

_____

_____

_____

8. Take credit for an idea that isn't really your own? _____

_____

_____

9. Read an editorial and then espouse the same point of view and use the same argument as the editorial writer when talking with your friends? (In writing, this is known as failing to give attribution.)

_____

_____

_____

10. Turn in a book report when you have only read a synopsis of the book?

_____

_____

_____

11. Let your friends "cut" in front of you while waiting in a long line to get into a theater?

_____

_____

_____

Name: _____ Date: _____

43. CHEATING (CONT.)

12. Force your way into the inside lane of traffic, because the outside lane is blocked ahead and therefore has almost no cars in it?

_____

_____

_____

B. Let's pursue the last two situations that are certainly common enough. What can you do about anyone who allows one or more friends to get into line ahead of you instead of going to the end of the line?

_____

_____

_____

_____

What are two other ways of handling the problem? _____

_____

_____

_____

How can you handle the situation of the person who zooms ahead in the empty outside lane and then forces his or her way into the inside lane, where people have patiently (or impatiently) been waiting, bumper-to-bumper to get past the snarl ahead?

_____

_____

_____

C. Do you think you might try one of these strategies the next time someone doesn't wait to take his or her turn in line?

_____

_____

Name: _____ Date: _____

44. BURGEONING BARRISTERS

Let's suppose that you live in a city of moderate size (about 200,000) and that you are a person of moderate means (neither wealthy nor deprived). Lately you have become aware of the increasing number of lawsuits in your city. There have been many instances of people suing physicians for malpractice, of individuals suing neighbors over property rights, and of both individuals and groups bringing suit against governmental agencies. At this time, you are not directly involved in any of these legal actions, but you have decided that part of the problem is a "copycat" mentality the people have in imitating others, especially when they seem to be successful in acquiring money quickly. In addition, you were looking through the yellow pages of the telephone book and noticed that there seems to be more pages devoted to listings for attorneys than there were in the last phone book. You become curious and start counting the number of attorneys in last year's telephone book and in this year's telephone book, and you find that there are 15% more listings in the current book. You are astonished.

No direct relationship can be established between what you perceive to be a considerable increase in civil suits in the courts and the increase in practicing lawyers in town, but you have a hunch that there really is a connection. Assuming that your hunch is correct, what can you expect in the future with regards to the burgeoning population of lawyers and the conditions of life in your city? What might happen if the number of lawyers continues to increase at the present rate?

1. How will recreational services (e.g., the maintenance of parks and the support of youth services) be affected?

   _____

   _____

2. Will the cost of medical services be affected? _____

   _____

3. Will there be more or fewer luxury cars sold? _____

   _____

4. Will there be an increase in the number of certified public accountants?

   _____

   _____

5. Will the enrollment of business and vocational schools be affected?

   _____

   _____

Name: _____ Date: _____

44. BURGEONING BARRISTERS (CONT.)

6. Will the dues for membership in the two local country clubs go up or down (or stay the same)?

_____

_____

7. Will the size of the police force remain the same or change? _____

_____

8. Will the profitability of the local postal service be affected? _____

_____

9. Will the price of newspapers change? _____

_____

10. Will there be more florists in the city?_____

_____

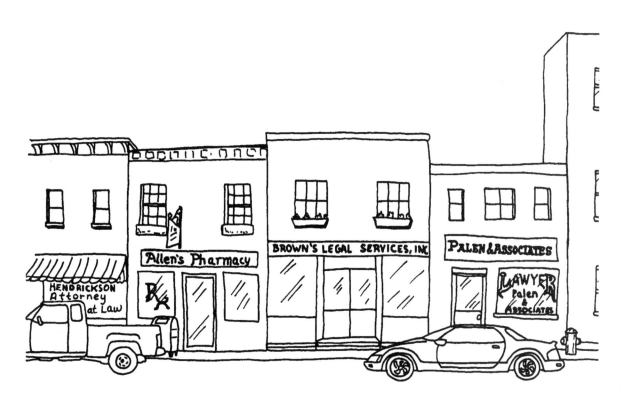

Name: _____ Date: _____

45. THE CLOWNS

In various democratic countries, people have elected poets, playwrights, actors, and other people from the arts and entertainment field to lead them. Actors and musicians have been governors, senators, and even President of the United States.

As far as we know, no governments have been run by comedians, although one humorist actually ran for president (Dick Gregory), and in the 1930s a number of people suggested that another (Will Rogers) run for the nation's highest office. Perhaps people think that someone who pokes fun at politicians and office holders wouldn't take the job of being the holder of a high office seriously enough.

1. Which comedian would make a marvelous congressman? _____

Why do you think so? _____

_____

2. Which comedian would make an excellent senator? _____

Why do you think so? _____

_____

3. Which comedian would make a good governor? _____

Why do you think so? _____

_____

4. Which comedian would make a fine president? _____

Why do you think so? _____

_____

5. What is the funniest thing you ever heard someone who holds an elected office say?

_____

_____

Name: _____ Date: _____

46. FOOLING THE FUZZ

A. We use a great many picturesque expressions in discussing crime and law enforcement. For example, we call a pickpocket a "dip," and a jail is known as a "slammer." Taking into consideration the number of books, movies, and television programs that feature criminals and police, we do a lot of thinking about the topic of crime. Along those lines, here are some questions to consider.

Is it wise to ...

1. fleece the police? _____ Why

   or why not? _____

   What would be the consequences if someone did fleece the police? _____

   _____

2. book a crook? _____ Why or why not? _____

   _____

   What would be the consequences if someone did book a crook? _____

   _____

3. hammer the slammer? _____ Why or why not? _____

   _____

   What would be the consequences if someone did hammer the slammer?

   _____

   _____

4. top a cop? _____ Why or why not? _____

   _____

   What would be the consequences if someone did top a cop? _____

   _____

5. slug a mug? _____ Why or why not? _____

   _____

Name: _____ Date: _____

46. FOOLING THE FUZZ (CONT.)

What would be the consequences if someone did slug a mug? _____

_____

6. trick a dick? _____ Why or why not? _____

_____

What would be the consequences if someone did trick a dick? _____

_____

7. fail a bail? _____ Why or why not? _____

_____

What would be the consequences if someone did fail a bail? _____

_____

8. grip a dip? _____ Why or why not? _____

_____

What would be the consequences if someone did grip a dip? _____

_____

9. nudge a judge? _____ Why or why not? _____

_____

What would be the consequences if someone did nudge a judge?

_____

_____

10. cajole a parole? _____ Why or why not? _____

_____

What would be the consequences if someone did cajole a parole?

_____

_____

B. On your own paper, see if you can come up with rhymes that deal with the ways in which people interact with nature. For instance, would it be advisable to trail a snail or to box a fox? Answer your own questions.

94

Name: _____ Date: _____

47. NO CONTEST!

A. People often talk about the evils of competition. They say that competition produces stress, heartbreak, greed, corruption, inequities, and iniquities of all kinds. However, a capitalistic society is based on competition. Without competition, there is no capitalism—meaning that our economy and our government could not exist. We even have laws encouraging competition and discouraging monopolies.

Maybe you think that for a variety of reasons you no longer want to compete with anyone or anything. Let's imagine that you have taken a solemn vow never to compete. Would your life change a great deal? In what ways would it change?

_____

_____

_____

_____

_____

B. Do animals compete among themselves? _____ Is there more competition between species, or within each species?

_____

_____

What are the major things for which animals compete? _____

_____

_____

Is there competition within a family or social group among ...

birds? _____   reptiles? _____   amphibians? _____

social insects? _____   primates? _____   marsupials? _____

marine mammals? _____

Name: _____ Date: _____

47. NO CONTEST! (CONT.)

C. Do plants compete? _____ How do they compete? _____

_____

_____

_____

Do plants ever compete with animals? _____ In what ways? _____

_____

_____

_____

In what ways do animals and plants compete with man? _____

_____

_____

_____

D. What are the benefits of competition? _____

_____

_____

_____

_____

_____

_____

_____

_____

Name: _____ Date: _____

48. TRUE OR FALSE?

We hear and read a lot of statements that make us wonder. Some of them seem outlandish, and others just seem unreasonable or unlikely. Now and then, we discover that a statement that seemed far-out just happens to be true—that what at first hearing or reading sounded ludicrous to us turns out to be correct.

A. The seven statements below are taken out of context. If you can, give each a context to explain why the statement could be true. If you can't imagine an appropriate context for a statement, then tell why it can't possibly be true.

1. Maizie was terribly ashamed of her name, and so now she calls herself "Tulip."

_____
_____
_____
_____
_____

2. Because of a spelling error, Melvin Smith wasn't able to vote in the election.

_____
_____
_____
_____
_____

3. Baseball season doesn't last as long as football season if you only have a tennis ball.

_____
_____
_____
_____
_____

Name: _____ Date: _____

48. TRUE OR FALSE? (CONT.)

4. Although she was old enough to be elected, she was too young to vote.

_____

_____

_____

_____

5. Many illiterate people find it easier to read comic books than to write letters.

_____

_____

_____

_____

_____

6. Once again, "Nobody" won the presidential election with the most votes.

_____

_____

_____

_____

7. Reporting national elections is like collecting speeding tickets in Nevada.

_____

_____

_____

_____

Name: _____ Date: _____

49. J.F.M.

Professor Asibov, an eminent historian at the state university, is a specialist in the period of U.S. history known as the Western Movement. By a great stroke of good luck, he was presented with a diary found in an attic by a woman whose forebears had come across the Oregon Trail and settled in Walla Walla, Washington. Eighteen men, women, and children crossed the plains in covered wagons drawn by horses and mules. One section of the diary, which was obviously written by a woman, is particularly gripping because it tells of a snowstorm in Utah that almost ended all of the lives of the members of the party. Four individuals, three adults and a child, didn't survive the ordeal.

The person who had the common sense and ingenuity that enabled most of the party to survive is only identified by the initials J.F.M. By advising the pioneers to preserve only items that were absolutely essential and to convert others to fuel and food, J.F.M. helped them avert freezing and starvation. Just as importantly, by locating game, watching the flight of birds, and observing the tracks of animals, J.F.M. advised the leaders of the party how they could get to a pass that would eventually lead them to a pasture and refuge from the punishing weather.

J.F.M. apparently traveled in a wagon with the writer of the diary, whom Professor Asibov could identify as the wife of P.T. and the mother of L.P.T. He could determine from a variety of clues that L.P.T. was a man—and probably not a very young one. Professor Asibov hypothesized that J.F.M. was L.P.T.'s brother or half-brother. Then he discovered that J.F.M couldn't have been a brother to L.P.T., because a reference was made to L.P.T. as being an only child.

Professor Asibov was quite perplexed. He was determined to identify this person whose intelligence had saved the lives of fourteen people. He decided to try another hypothesis, namely that J.F.M. was P.T.'s brother and therefore the writer's brother-in-law. There was a reference to J.F.M.'s knowledge of guns, but a thorough examination of the diary showed that J.F.M. wasn't one of the men who had defended the wagon train when it was attacked by a small band of Indians. It seemed to the professor that if J.F.M. were an able-bodied man, he would have been among the men defending the party.

"Could J.F.M. have been an Indian himself?" wondered Professor Asibov. Maybe J.F.M. came along as a guide. But the professor discarded that notion as preposterous because J.F.M. traveled with the other three in the wagon and shared their customs and beliefs.

Who was J.F.M.? Why do you think so? _____

_____

_____

_____

_____

_____

_____

Name: _____   Date: _____

50. WASTING AWAY

Waste is something virtually unknown in nature. On the other hand, the concept of waste is an important one in man's world. We have many, many kinds of waste in our society. One of the most spectacular—and harmful—is the spilling of oil by a tanker at sea. But waste is found on a much smaller scale more often. We throw away many articles that might be reused or utilized in other ways, as in the case of metal bottle caps, eggshells, and dried-up ballpoint pens.

How can these be put to use and not wasted?

1. leaves from trees _____

_____

2. orange peels _____

_____

3. dandelions _____

_____

4. metal bottle caps _____

_____

5. ugly neckties _____

_____

6. dead flashlight batteries _____

_____

7. broken dishes _____

_____

Name: _____   Date: _____

50. WASTING AWAY (CONT.)

8. dried-up ballpoint pens _____

_____

9. manual typewriters _____

_____

10. automobile tires _____

_____

11. "junk" mail _____

_____

12. time spent waiting in line _____

_____

13. compassion _____

_____

Which features do all of these waste problems have in common?

_____

_____

_____

_____

101

Name: _____ Date: _____

51. MUSIC ON THE JOB

A. Where does music help, and where does it hinder? Music can soothe, annoy, excite, and inspire—and much, much more. What kind of music would disrupt the following people when they are carrying out their jobs?

1. a paramedic going to a residence in an ambulance at 2:00 A.M. _____

2. a free-lance writer the day before a deadline _____

3. a skipper of a fishing vessel that takes people out to sea to fish for marlin and swordfish

    _____

4. a high school physics teacher with a class of eleventh graders during last period on a Friday afternoon

    _____

5. a worker in an automobile manufacturing assembly plant on Monday morning _____

6. a person selling notions in a department store on Monday morning _____

7. a young lady who delivers messages on her bicycle in New York City on Wednesday afternoon

    _____

8. a bus driver with a full load of passengers on Sunday morning 45 minutes from the next stop in Montana _____

9. a street cleaner working the main street of a city on July 5 after an Independence Day parade _____

10. a taxi driver on Saturday afternoon without a fare _____

11. a dental assistant cleaning a woman's teeth on the day after Thanksgiving

    _____

B. Now go back and try very hard to find a situation in which music would be very helpful to each of the eleven workers. What kind of music would it be?

1. a paramedic going to a residence in an ambulance at 2:00 A.M. _____

2. a free-lance writer the day before a deadline _____

Name: _____ Date: _____

51. MUSIC ON THE JOB (CONT.)

3. a skipper of a fishing vessel that takes people out to sea to fish for marlin and swordfish
_____

4. a high school physics teacher with a class of eleventh graders during last period on a Friday afternoon _____

5. a worker in an automobile manufacturing assembly plant on Monday morning
_____

6. a person selling notions in a department store on Monday morning
_____

7. a young lady who delivers messages on her bicycle in New York City on Wednesday afternoon _____

8. a bus driver with a full load of passengers on Sunday morning 45 minutes from the next stop in Montana _____

9. a street cleaner working the main street of a city on July 5 after an Independence Day parade _____

10. a taxi driver on Saturday afternoon without a fare _____

11. a dental assistant cleaning a woman's teeth on the day after Thanksgiving
_____

C. Can you imagine a situation for a worker in which he or she is helped tremendously by music, but everyone else is put off by it?

_____

What might that situation be? _____

_____

_____

D. In what situations could music help you but at present it either isn't available or you aren't using it?

_____

_____

Name: _____ Date: _____

52. THE THINGS PEOPLE SAY

People say nice things to you—or not-so-nice things to you—every day. You like to hear the nice things, of course, but you don't like to hear the bad things. Most of all, you don't like to be bossed around. But there are other things people say that are not good, nor are they bad, and they aren't bossing anyone.

A. Would you like to be told that you will be an average worker when you grow up? _____ Why or why not? _____
_____
_____
_____

B. Would you like to be told that you should never lose a button? _____
Why or why not? _____
_____
_____
_____

C. Would you like someone to say that you are going to learn another language when you grow up? _____ Why or why not? _____
_____
_____
_____

D. Would you like someone to tell you that you don't make more grammatical mistakes than most people? _____ Why or why not? _____
_____
_____
_____

E. Would you like someone to say that he or she wouldn't mind very much if you decide to switch your political party? _____ Why or why not? _____
_____
_____
_____

Name: _____ Date: _____

53. BLACK OR BLUE?

A. Jon likes to do sketches in ink. His sketches are unusual, though, because he uses only two colors—black and blue. Recently, he bought three bottles of ink, two of black ink and one of blue. So he would know where to get them quickly, he put them in a little box that was just big enough to hold them.

The tops of the bottles are identical, and so when Jon reaches into the box for a bottle of ink, he sometimes pulls out blue when he wants black. In fact, it seems that he usually pulls out blue instead of black, even though there are two bottles of black and only one of blue.

What suggestion do you have for Jon so that he'll always get a black or a blue when he wants that particular color?

_____

_____

_____

_____

_____

_____

_____

_____

B. Can you apply the same principle for solving Jon's problem to another problem? The problem might be one of situating people, furniture, buildings, trucks, trains, or almost anything else. Draw a diagram of your idea.

Name: _____   Date: _____

54. GREED

Scene #1

A thin, poorly dressed man reaches nervously into his pocket and pulls out several coins. He impulsively pushes them across the counter to a young salesman, who carefully picks up each coin and places it on a black velvet cloth. The young man adjusts an eye loupe to his right eye.

As he does so, the unkempt man emits a little sound from lips that are pulled tightly against his yellowing teeth. Then, impatiently, he blurts, "What'll ya give me for 'em?"

"I'd have to check with Mr. Newman, but they look genuine ... At least five thousand, I would guess."

As the young man pronounces the last syllable, the thin man reaches out and snatches the coins off the cloth, chuckles, and wheels around and darts through the doors of the shop.

Scene #2

Skipping happily and singing a television jingle to herself, the five-year-old is enjoying her day at the beach with her mother.

"Ho! Another one!" she exclaims as she stops and picks up a glittering shell in the sand. Her mother smiles broadly.

"And another!" the girl cries delightedly.

A half-hour later, the child reaches for one more shell, scoops it up, and thrusts it at her mother.

"I just don't have any more room in my pockets, honey. I'm afraid we can't take any more."

"Oh, Mommy, you <u>have</u> to!" insists the girl. "It's so pretty!"

"You really have enough shells, dear. I don't know what we're going to do with all of them," her mother replies a little impatiently.

"No-no-no! I see a big one!"

Scene #3

The tour guide informs the group that the scheduled events are at an end for the day.

"It's only 8:30," a large, middle-aged man whispers loudly to his small, fashionably dressed wife. "We're getting gypped! We can still see the National Palace. They don't close until 9:30. And then we can see the shops on that street somebody talked about yesterday."

Name: _____ Date: _____

54. GREED (CONT.)

"You're exactly right, Homer," responds the woman. "And I don't think he's scheduled anything in the morning until 9:15. Who wants to go to Mexico and sleep the whole day! I've heard the best time to go to the Farmers Market is around 6:00. We can be there for an hour, get to that cafe by 7:30 or so, and the artists will probably have their paintings displayed in that park near the hotel before 8:30."

A. In these three little scenes, which of the individuals is being greedy? _____

_____

_____

_____

B. If any are exhibiting that trait, what are they greedy for? _____

_____

_____

_____

_____

_____

_____

_____

_____

> Obsessed,
> with More,
> a craving that
> steals from the heart—
> Greed.

Mostly we think of greed in terms of money, but we can be greedy about many other things. Are you greedy for anything? Affection? Excitement? Books? CDs? Clothes? Money? Knowledge? Power? Food? New experiences? Life?

Does greed imply <u>too much</u>—more than enough for the average person? Can you be greedy if you don't have as much as others, or as much as the average person in your situation?

Name: _____ Date: _____

C. How does greed pay off or not pay off? Write at least three paragraphs arguing for or against a certain kind of greed. We might remind you that a paragraph has these features:

1. It has a topic sentence that leads off the paragraph and tells what the paragraph is about.
2. That topic is then developed. You can list details; cite incidents or examples; compare items; give reasons, causes, results, or effects; and/or describe the steps in a process.
3. These sentences are arranged so that the reader can move easily from one sentence to the next.
4. A concluding sentence summarizes or ties together the ideas expressed in the paragraph.

You can use the space below to sketch out the ideas for your argument.

_____

_____

_____

_____

_____

_____

_____

_____

_____

_____

_____

_____

_____

Name: _____ Date: _____

55. USING IT UP

We hear a great deal about the depletion of the world's supply of oil; it is undoubtedly a serious problem. But other things are growing scarce, and some of them are more important than oil. Among them are enough food for the starving people of the world, uncontaminated water, and forests.

In some states, schools benefit from revenues that are derived from timber harvests on public lands, so a tremendous scarcity of harvestable timber would directly affect those schools.

1. What would happen if those funds are no longer available to schools dependent upon timber sales?

    _____

    _____

    _____

    _____

    _____

2. What would be the consequences for all schools of a tremendous shortage of wood products? List as many consequences as you can think of.

    _____

    _____

    _____

    _____

    _____

    _____

Name: _____ Date: _____

56. SPOILING A TREASURE

Khao Yai, Thailand's first national park, is a watershed for four major rivers, a habitat to many rare animal species, a bastion of genetic biodiversity, and an important center for education and recreation. Just outside this park is an area that has been almost completely deforested, where villages are poor, and many people are landless. The result of having a national park next to impoverished people is that the villagers are using the forest in the park for illegal logging and hunting.

The villagers have been arrested and punished for encroaching on the park and for poaching, but they haven't desisted. In addition, the government has vigorously tried to educate the people about the preciousness of this national treasure, but there is a good deal of evidence to support the claim that empty stomachs make these efforts irrelevant to the villagers' needs. The problem is getting worse by the day; no attempt at solving it has come close to working.

A different approach is necessary to stop the depredation of the park. What program can you suggest? On your own paper, using all of the information you have about this problem that exists in many parts of the world, try to break free of the conventional approaches in order to come up with a viable solution. First, jot down your ideas in the space below.

_____

_____

_____

_____

_____

_____

_____

_____

_____

_____

Name: _____ Date: _____

57. SLEUTHING

A. A prominent bit of lore concerning indigenous Americans pertains to their remarkable ability to track animals by looking at various kinds of evidence that could be seen in and on the earth after one or more animals had been traveling, grazing, preying on other animals, etc. The term is sometimes used for the kind of detective work called "reading the clues." We do a different kind of sleuthing today, and we usually benefit from finding—and understanding—various kinds of clues. There are many ways in which we obtain important information, but we may not always be aware that we are picking up clues and cues. For instance, if you have a pet, you undoubtedly have picked up bits of information about its health from observing its behavior—listlessness and lying around, drooping head, dry nose, certain noises, and the like.

B. Here are some common questions you might have as you go through a typical school day. How do you generally go about gaining the information needed to answer each question?

1. What is the weather like as you awake in the morning? What are the clues?

_____

_____

2. If you aren't preparing breakfast, how do you determine whether or not you should be eager to get to the table?

_____

_____

3. What is the mood of the first person you meet in the morning?

_____

_____

4. At school, should you ask questions in your least favorite class today? What are the clues?

_____

_____

5. Should you be careful not to bring up any touchy subject today with your best friend?

_____

_____

Name: _____   Date: _____

57. SLEUTHING (CONT.)

6. Should you have a second helping at lunch? What are the external and internal clues?

_____

_____

7. Is this a good day to study hard? What are the external and internal clues?

_____

_____

_____

C. What are the advantages of the kind of sleuthing called for in the questions above?

_____

_____

_____

_____

_____

What are the disadvantages? _____

_____

_____

_____

_____

_____

_____

_____

Name: _____ Date: _____

58. GRATUITOUS GIFTS

A. People seem to be compelled to give gifts to heads of state—presidents, prime ministers, and kings. Movie and television stars also receive a wide variety of gifts, mostly unwanted. Most of what is given is of doubtful value or usefulness to the recipients, e.g., flags, quilts, carved figures, guns with silver bullets, etc.

In some way or other, each of the givers sees his or her gift as an appropriate one to send to the recipient. There are times when the person receiving the gift is undoubtedly surprised and amused by the present. Dwight Eisenhower received three newspaper photographs—of himself, his wife, and Johnny Cash, framed by a chain of folded cigarette packs.

Instead of truly eminent people, perhaps more gifts should be given to the unsung heroes of the world. What would be appropriate gifts for these people?

1. a person who, with his or her own funds, sets up an animal hospital for injured and abandoned animals

   _____

   _____

2. a Coast Guard crew that regularly rescues weekend fishermen in stormy weather

   _____

   _____

3. street cleaners _____

   _____

4. letter carriers who really do deliver the mail in rain, sleet, and snow

   _____

   _____

Name: _____ Date: _____

58. GRATUITOUS GIFTS (CONT.)

5. workers who unplug sewer drains after heavy rains _____

_____

6. volunteers who help school children cross busy intersections _____

_____

7. linemen who restore electrical power after power lines have been broken

_____

_____

8. volunteers in literacy programs for illiterate adults _____

_____

9. people who work with multi-handicapped children _____

_____

10. clerks at all-night grocery stores _____

_____

B. Now select one of those appropriate gifts for an unsung hero and make it (a) more long-lasting, (b) more attractive than it ordinarily is, and (c) more practical and/or useful. How would you accomplish each of these goals, given a reasonable amount of money and time?

_____

_____

_____

_____

_____

_____

Name: _____ Date: _____

59. POISON

A. Did you know that the poinsettia, our favorite Christmas plant, is poisonous? So are the elderberry and horse-chestnut. Many things that we live with every day can be quite harmful if we eat them or are exposed to them in certain ways. Most often we are not injured by the poisons around us; but occasionally they become concentrated so that we are adversely affected—as in the case of the deadly smogs that have struck down hundreds of people in large cities such as London.

If you are poisoned, very often the right antidote can save your life. What poisons are you frequently exposed to?

B. What makes something a poison? _____

_____

Is milk a poison? _____ How might milk be a poison? _____

_____

C. What is the antidote for each of these poisons?

1. arsenic _____

2. ptomaine _____

3. nicotine _____

4. Do you know the usual antidote for rat poison? _____ (If you don't, you should find out.)

5. Do you know an effective remedy for poison oak or poison ivy? _____ (If you don't, you should find out.)

D. What would be your special antidote for these insidious social poisons?

1. envy _____

2. hate _____

3. prejudice _____

4. fear _____

5. bitterness _____

6. self-pity _____

E. Explain one of your suggested antidotes for one of the social poisons by writing a short essay or a story on your own paper that features the all-too-familiar kinds of human poisons that cripple us morally and spiritually.

Name: _____ Date: _____

60. WHAT DO YOU SEE?

A. Take a good look at the lines at the right. What
do they make you think of?

_____

_____

B. Now rotate this piece of paper 90° and look at
the lines again. Does a different image emerge,
one that you could easily complete by adding
lines? Write down what you see now.

_____

_____

_____

C. What if you rotate the page another 90° and look at the lines again? What different image
do you get now? Write it down.

_____

D. Finally, rotate this page another 90° and find out what you can see. Write this down.

_____

Now examine the different images you have seen.

Which one do you like best? _____

Which one do you think is the most unusual? _____

_____

Which one is the most exciting? _____

_____

On your own paper, draw the one that appeals most to you by adding as many lines and
colors as you'd like.

E. Why don't you look into the troublesome problem of the rights of landowners versus the
efforts of the federal government to preserve wetlands? Apply the principle of looking at
something from several different angles. Aside from the viewpoints of the landowners and
the federal government, what other interested groups have a stake in this ongoing dispute?

Name: _____ Date: _____

61. SHOCKING

A. *Shock* is the medical term for a sudden change in a person's physical functioning. It can be brought about by bodily trauma; electrical shocks and burns frequently bring about shock to people. More often, the word *shock* is used to describe the reaction of someone who has experienced a great surprise. What is the difference between getting a surprise and getting a shock? What must be present in the event if there is to be genuine shock?

_____

_____

_____

_____

_____

_____

B. Most of the time we think of shocks as events that are negative in character, as when we get some terrible news, but you can also have very pleasant shocks. Which of these events would produce genuine shock in you? Explain why.

1. A high grade on a test when you expected a lower grade _____

_____

2. A close call when a car almost hits you _____

_____

3. No one bawls you out when you rip your best pair of pants _____

_____

4. The governor dies of a heart attack _____

_____

Name: _____   Date: _____

61. SHOCKING (CONT.)

C. You may have heard the expression, "That shocked him into his senses." What kind of shock could bring someone to her or his senses?

Explain how you could be shocked into your senses in each of these situations:

1. not getting chosen _____

_____

_____

2. getting chosen _____

_____

_____

3. finding money in your pocket _____

_____

_____

4. not finding money in your pocket _____

_____

_____

5. being terribly insulted _____

_____

_____

6. not being terribly insulted when you expected to be _____

_____

_____

D. What shock would give you the greatest pleasure? _____

_____

What would be your reactions to that shock? _____

_____

Name: _____ Date: _____

A. This is a story of a mother whose son almost quit school because of a locker. Before his first day in junior high school, the boy and his mother visited the school. His mother thought it would be an especially good idea since they had just moved into town. The boy learned that all students had their own lockers, and he was given the number of his locker and its combination. His mother suggested that they examine his locker because on the first day of the following week, he would have to be able to open it. Having never opened a locker with a combination lock, the boy was apprehensive. Sure enough, he wasn't able to open the lock. His mother helped him, and they finally were able to open the lock. Over the weekend, the boy's thoughts of school were poisoned by the fear that he wouldn't be able to open his locker on Monday.

When the terrible day arrived, he reached his locker a half-hour before the bell was to ring for the first class and struggled with the combination lock for several minutes. When the other students crowded around him, opening up their lockers, he gave up and went to class. In the first three periods, he was given three textbooks and three assignments. During the noon recess, he tried unsuccessfully to open his locker again. Red-faced, he went to the office to make sure he had the correct combination. The assistant principal accompanied the boy to his locker to make certain that the lock was operating correctly; it was. He put his books into the locker and went to lunch. After the noon hour ended, however, he couldn't open the locker. He went home in a very dejected state of mind.

After telling his mother about his inability to open the locker, the boy went to his room, but he couldn't do his homework lessons because his books were in his locker at school. When his teachers asked for the completed assignments on Tuesday, the boy wasn't able to hand anything in to them. He went home in an awful state of depression. "Why don't you have another student help you?" his mother asked when she learned of her son's plight. The boy said he would ask someone, but because he hadn't made any friends at school as yet, he knew he wouldn't.

On Wednesday, he was embarrassed when two of his teachers asked the students to read sections from their textbooks, and his were still in his locker. The young man thought about going to the assistant principal again, but he couldn't bring himself to ask the man for help. The assistant principal hadn't been exactly unfriendly when he'd assisted the boy before, but he hadn't been particularly kind either. The boy's only thoughts that evening were of never going to school again.

When his mother came home from work, she knew immediately that her son hadn't been able to open his locker. The door to his room was closed, and there was no mess in the kitchen. Being an understanding woman, she didn't press him about the problem at dinner. After considerable thought that evening, she came up with a plan. She would rehearse the

Name: _____   Date: _____

62. LOCKED OUT (CONT.)

working of his combination lock with her son at home until the whole operation was second nature to him. She cut out two pieces of cardboard, wrote numbers on the larger piece, and put them together with a pin, making something that would work like a combination lock. After a good deal of coaxing, the boy consented to practice moving the small piece of cardboard to the numbers on the larger piece, following the sequence of numbers on a now-crumpled piece of paper. His mother discovered his problem—he was turning it clockwise when he should be turning it counter-clockwise, and vice versa.

Now there was only one more thing the woman could do to help her son, but it was risky. Nevertheless, at 6:30 A.M., she drove him to school. Except for a back door leading from the main building to the playground, all of the doors were locked. The custodian was in the boiler room having a cup of coffee, so he didn't see a lady and a boy furtively enter the building from the rear and head for the lockers in the hall. With his mother watching anxiously, the boy opened his lock the first time. Relieved, she went back home to have a second cup of coffee. He took out his books and went to the restroom.

B. Is it more embarrassing to be unable to open a locker in the gym than in the main building?

_____ Why or why not? _____

_____

_____

When you think of a locker, what comes to your mind? _____

_____

Would schools be better if they didn't have lockers? _____

Why do you think so? _____

_____

C. Most of us have had an embarrassing experience with an inanimate object such as a lock, household appliance, bicycle, television set, or other gadget. Maybe you can recall such an incident that you or someone you know had. Why don't you write a brief story about that experience? You can either write it in the first person, using "I," "me," etc.; or you can give the embarrassed person a fictitious name. On your own paper, outline the main parts of your story, and then write your story.

120

Name: _____ Date: _____

63. RELAXED TENSION

A. Some authorities contend that the secret to both athletic and intellectual success is "relaxed tension." On the face of it, you might suppose that this is more double-talk by people who want to sound important. When a person is tense, how can he or she also be relaxed?

Actually, the notion makes sense if you consider that when an individual is at ease but ready to react, he or she is in exactly the right condition to leap over a high-jump bar or to write a good examination paper. It's a matter of balancing two opposites, of reconciling two opposing forces in your makeup. If you are too tense, or too relaxed, you won't do well on the examination, nor will you clear the high-jump bar. This same principle holds true in social situations. If you are alert but not "tied-up," you are more likely to make a good impression on others. So all of us really are engaged in the business of reconciling opposites in our natures most of the time.

Let's investigate several other apparent contradictions that might be quite plausible when considered from a certain point of view. See if you can explain how each of these expressions might make sense.

1. little giant _____

_____

2. clearly confusing _____

_____

3. serious nonsense _____

_____

4. silent cheering _____

_____

5. tolerant bigot _____

_____

6. tuneless song _____

_____

B. Sometimes, we say one thing and do another. For example, we say it is awful to gossip, but we enjoy it so much we wouldn't think of giving up gossiping. Even our government

Name: _____ Date: _____

63. RELAXED TENSION (CONT.)

engages in contradictory behavior—at the same time the tobacco industry is subsidized, the Surgeon General requires warnings about the hazards of smoking, and cigarette advertising is banned from television.

Can you see any contradictions in your own behavior? If so, what are they?

_____

_____

What is society doing now that doesn't make sense for a healthy and prosperous future?

_____

_____

Can you think of what we are doing that is not in our own best interest regarding:

1. international espionage? _____

_____

_____

2. the purchase of smaller corporations by larger ones? _____

_____

_____

3. public health? _____

_____

_____

4. the consumption of fossil fuels? _____

_____

_____

5. the consumption of other fuels? _____

_____

_____

If you can't think of ways we are acting unwisely in any of these areas, read some national periodicals and ask people who are well-informed about what is happening in the world.

122

Name: _____ Date: _____

64. EMOTION

A. Although our emotions can get us into trouble some-times, life would be awfully dull if it were devoid of emotion. If you saw and heard someone describing an umpire's bad decision, the death of a pet, a new television program, the first lovely day of spring, a newborn baby's looks, or a fight, you would surely be able to detect some feelings or emotions in what you saw and heard. It would be quite remarkable if you didn't.

Can you think of any event that can be described without any emotion being revealed on the part of the speaker?

_____

B. When you think of the governor, what feelings do you have?

_____

_____

_____

When you think of the mayor, what feelings do you have? _____

_____

_____

When you think of the president, what feelings do you have? _____

_____

_____

C. When should there be <u>more</u> emotion in government? Explain. _____

_____

_____

When should there be <u>less</u> emotion in government? Explain. _____

_____

_____

Name: _____   Date: _____

65. OCCUPATIONAL EVOLUTION

A. Many jobs have disappeared, and many others have appeared in the last century. In large part, these changes have taken place because of advances in technology. Among the jobs that no longer exist are those of the iceman delivering chunks of ice from a truck and messengers delivering telegrams on a bicycle. With the introduction of refrigerators, people no longer had any use for iceboxes—they are sold as antiques now. Messengers on bicycles were replaced first by people delivering telegrams in cars, and then by people in offices sending the telegrams by telephone and mail.

B. Undoubtedly, many more jobs will disappear in the future, and many others will be created. Why don't you do some guessing about how the job market will evolve? Here are six occupations that have changed during the past three generations. What will they become in the future?

When your grandparents were born	When you were born	When your children are born
1. radio repairman	TV technician	_____
2. cobbler	worker in a shoe factory	_____
3. streetcar conductor	bus driver	_____
4. radio actor	TV actor	_____
5. peddler of household goods	door-to-door salesman of cooking utensils	_____
6. typist	word processor	_____

C. What other jobs will cease to exist when your children are the same age as you are now?

_____

_____

_____

_____